UNSCALABLE

UNSCALABLE
UNORTHODOX STARTUP GROWTH STORIES

CHARLIE GUO

INKSHARES

Copyright © 2016 Charlie Guo

All rights reserved.

No part of this book may be reproduced, or stored in a retrieval system, or transmitted in any form or by any means, electronic, mechanical, photocopying, recording, or otherwise, without express written permission of the publisher.

Published by Inkshares, Inc., San Francisco, California

www.inkshares.com

Edited and designed by Girl Friday Productions

www.girlfridayproductions.com

Cover design by Jason Ramirez

©mw2st/Shutterstock

ISBN: 9781941758557

e-ISBN: 9781941758564

Library of Congress Control Number: 2015942395

First edition

Printed in the United States of America

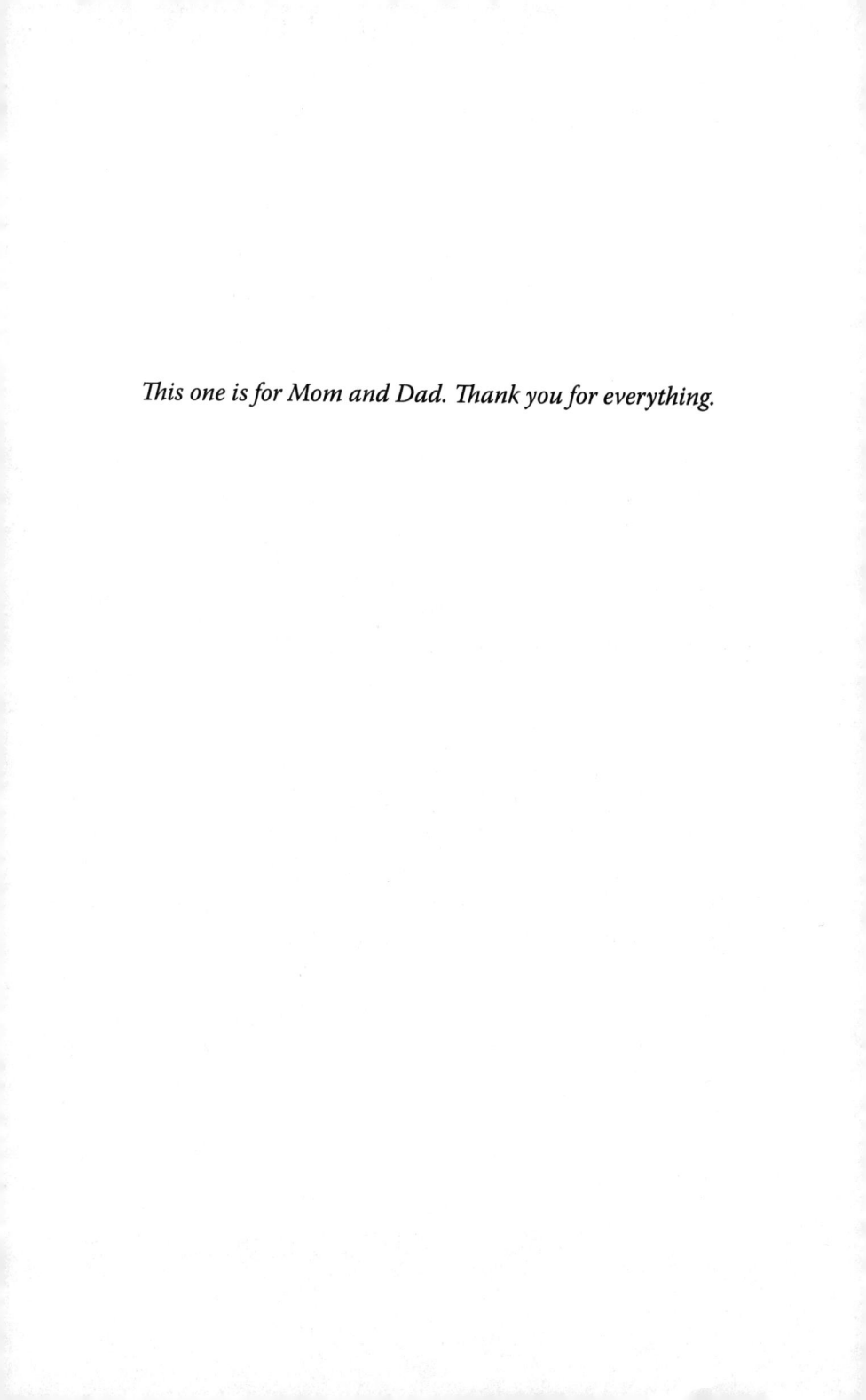

This one is for Mom and Dad. Thank you for everything.

CONTENTS

Introduction. 1
1. Teleborder (James Richards) 3
2. General Assembly (Brad Hargreaves) 15
3. Crowdbooster (Ricky Yean). 24
4. FlightCar (Rujul Zaparde) 34
5. Tilt (James Beshara) 42
6. Verbling (Jake Jolis) 50
7. DoorDash (Tony Xu) 59
8. inDinero (Jessica Mah) 70
9. Zenefits (Parker Conrad) 77
10. ZeroCater (Arram Sabeti). 88
11. Teespring (Walker Williams) 95
12. Codecademy (Ryan Bubinski) 104
13. 99dresses (Nikki Durkin) 112
14. Watsi (Grace Garey) 120
15. GitHub (Tom Preston-Werner). 128
Acknowledgments 141
About the Author. 143
Glossary 145
List of Patrons 149

INTRODUCTION

In the last twenty years, the costs of starting a technology company have plummeted. Projects that previously required tens of thousands of dollars and hundreds of hours of effort can now be done in a weekend with a credit card.

In the mainstream, the image of a tech founder has gone from nerd to "rockstar" (e.g., Aaron Sorkin's *The Social Network* or Mike Judge's *Silicon Valley*). Silicon Valley, home to Google, Apple, Twitter, Facebook, and countless other tech startups, remains the hot spot for those attempting to take a good idea and turn it into a success story.

In the last few years alone, startup accelerators have fueled this diversity even further, each one helping dozens of companies launch every few months. Y Combinator (YC) is the most prestigious accelerator of them all; it has incubated hundreds of companies (a few of which are in this book) from their earliest days, including tech juggernauts like Dropbox and Airbnb.

The one thing all of these companies have in common, even the juggernauts, is the emotional roller coaster that is the startup life. Going from the top of the world to the brink of failure, often within days or weeks, is standard for early-stage technology companies.

Every company has to do something crazy or unorthodox when it's young; that's just part of being scrappy. Paul Graham, the cofounder of YC, explains this counterintuitive nature of launching:

> Startups take off because the founders make them take off. There may be a handful that just grew by themselves, but usually it takes some sort of push to get them going. A good metaphor would be the cranks that car engines had before they got electric starters. Once the engine was going, it would keep going, but there was a separate and laborious process to get it going.[1]

Unfortunately, these stories aren't often told. Much of the tech press focuses on the mythology of the founders or rewrites the company history into a seemingly overnight success. Instead, I wanted to find out about the unglamorous, the unsexy, the unscalable techniques.

The stories in this book about seemingly unscalable strategies show commonalities among very, very diverse companies. Some are several years old, some are dead, some are tiny, some are worth billions of dollars, some are complete unknowns, and some are household names.

This collection of interviews with several of the most promising companies impacting the world of tech is meant for anyone interested in how unscalable ideas lie at the core of the products and services that change the way we live.

---

1. "Do Things That Don't Scale," Paul Graham, July 2013, http://paulgraham.com/ds.html.

CHAPTER 1: TELEBORDER

James Richards, Cofounder & CEO

The youngest of our companies, Teleborder, was started in 2013 by James Richards and Michael Smith. It began as a legal services marketplace; however, the company was unable to find product-market fit and pivoted to its current product, a tool to hire and manage international employees. Pivots like this are fairly common among startups; many companies are the result of pivots, including some now-famous businesses like Instagram and Twitter.

Pivots are sometimes looked down upon, but they often reveal the tenacity of the founders. Luck plays an enormous role in the success of a startup, and although it's never easy, it's important to listen to the users (or the lack thereof) and try different strategies when necessary.

In deciding to change tracks, the founders of Teleborder experienced a problem often encountered by young, smart founders: being intelligent and building a product aren't enough to disrupt an entrenched market. Many founders, especially technical ones, underestimate the importance of having strong marketing and distribution channels. Teleborder learned this lesson the hard way, but the founders took the lesson to heart and have built their current product one user at a time, collecting feedback and iterating on their product along the way.

GUO: I know Teleborder was a pivot, but I'd love to go back to the beginning. How did you get started?

RICHARDS: Sure. So I'm a lawyer. Michael, my cofounder at the time, was not a lawyer, but he hated lawyers because he'd had to deal with them a few times. And the worst part about dealing with lawyers was always feeling like you're getting screwed on bills. Lawyers are very, very expensive. They're also very opaque when it comes to pricing. It's rare that you can look up on a website how much a particular service costs. Although intuitively it seemed like you should be able to ask, "How much will it cost me to get my company set up?" or "How much will it cost me to get this transaction done?"—but you couldn't. It just seemed like you ought to be able to tell somebody how much a legal service ought to cost, at least within some sort of range. But no one did.

So we thought, what if we could package law into these little fixed-price nuggets that you could buy just as easily as buying a book off of Amazon, and get all of the same things, like price, clarity, fungibility, certainty, returns, all of that stuff? If you could basically e-commercify law, it would be a lot better, right? Because I wouldn't have to pick up the phone and call a lawyer and talk for an hour and interview ten of them and get screwed on bills. I'd just click a button to magically get a lawyer and it would be that price. So that was the idea.

GUO: How did you get your first customers?

RICHARDS: Well, that was the problem. We actually never had customers, which was why we needed to pivot. It was a two-sided marketplace, and we started by thinking, "Well, if lawyers are our inventory, the first thing we should do is go get some lawyers." And so we went out and, in fairness, we did a pretty good job of getting lawyers. I don't know the exact number, but we had on the order of a couple thousand lawyers on our wait list, and we had onboarded a couple hundred.

Actually, we didn't try everything. We tried virtually nothing. We were still in the "we are geniuses" mode, trying to make things superscalable from day one.

By the time YC interviews rolled around, we had lawyers who we interviewed, who we screened, who basically signed up to offer services on our site—and more than just signing up and giving us an email address, actually picked the services that they wanted to offer. So we would have, I don't know, let's say incorporation—I can't remember what our actual services were, but we'd have an incorporation service—and we would set the price, say $500, and we'd set what was included in that package, and then lawyers would log in and they had this dashboard where they could opt in to offering those services. And so we onboarded on the order of several hundred lawyers and had several thousand waiting to get on. Which I think is what made YC go, "Oh, these seem like smart, determined guys, and lawyers don't think it's crazy!"

In terms of how we got [lawyers], Craigslist was surprisingly good. There's an alarmingly high number of lawyers trawling Craigslist. It's Craigslist, so you get what you get, but there are some good ones there. And an initial seed is good enough to have them tell their friends. Because lawyers, like any service provider, are selling time. And time is the most perishable of inventory because it literally disappears every second. So when lawyers hang out, they all talk about how to get more clients. So if you can get a bunch of lawyers excited about something, then they'll all just sign up in droves.

But that's not the hard part. We should have known it, but we were really arrogant. We thought, "Oh, look at all these lawyers signing up; clearly we're so smart," when actually they were signing up because that's the easy part. The hard part is actually getting clients. And they were signing up because they thought we would solve that problem for them, whereas we thought that by having them, that would solve our problem of getting clients. We were both looking at each other to solve each other's problem.

It's so ironic, and in hindsight, so stupid. We launched our customer-facing side the morning of our YC interview, mainly because we didn't want to walk in and say, "We have no sales, and we haven't launched our customer-facing side yet." At least we had one of those two things. It was like, "We have no sales, but you can't blame us because we launched thirty minutes ago." And we spent all of May, June, and July trying everything to get customers. By July we were grasping at straws.

GUO: What were some of the things that you tried?

RICHARDS: Actually, we didn't try everything. We tried virtually nothing. We were still in the "we are geniuses" mode, trying to make things superscalable from day one. We launched every vertical of law I could think of, between ten and twenty verticals of law. And we had lawyers in the top fifty or so metropolitan areas in the United States. We thought, "We're going to do this big-bang launch" and "If it's e-commerce, the way to do e-commerce is simple: you just get people coming to your website, then a certain percentage of them will convert, and that's your company. If we get a hundred visitors, five of them will buy, right? It's just math."

To get visitors, we did a bunch of SEO [search engine optimization] things, like we had custom landing pages for every type of law, in every major metropolitan area, that we generated programmatically. We had a newsletter that no one ever signed up to. The thinking was something like, "People will sign up for this newsletter, then we'll email them stuff, and then a couple years later they'll buy a legal service from us." In hindsight, it was really bad.

We tried all the things that in theory were scalable, but mainly SEO and trying to get large numbers of people to visit our site. And you know, we were successful in getting people to visit our site; our Google Analytics numbers went up, and at first we thought that was awesome. But those visits never converted into sales. Each week our excuse for not having any sales was "We just need more visitors. Last week we only had a thousand, now we have three thousand. Now we have eight thousand." And when it got to ten thousand visitors per week, and there was still nobody buying, we said, "All right, it's a large enough sample size; now we have a problem. We have a real problem."

Looking back, we should have picked one area of law rather than twenty, and picked one, not even necessarily urban, just one area of the world, geographically speaking, as opposed to the top fifty metropolitan areas in the United States. And we should have owned that market, whatever it was. But instead we did the precise opposite, which was to try to go as big as possible, and it was a bit like putting a drop of ink in the ocean: it got diluted to the point of oblivion; it just didn't matter. All our efforts just didn't matter.

GUO: So at this point, you decided to pivot. What did that process look like for you guys?

RICHARDS: We'd been thinking about it for a few days; obviously when the numbers are that bad and Demo Day is approaching, you start to really worry. We still thought we were geniuses and that there was some sort of trick to getting customers even though YC had consistently told us there wasn't. We just didn't listen.

So we finally decided to go talk to Paul Graham [PG] about this. And I kind of expected PG to pull a Yoda and tell us, "Okay, yeah, here's the secret, go do this. Change the color of this button and the users will come." Of course, instead he told us, "You guys need to go do precisely the opposite of what you've been doing.

Clearly we had a business, because we made more money in one day than our legal marketplace made in one year, but we didn't know how to go from $3,000 to $30,000, and $30,000 to $300,000, and so on.

You should (1) pick *one* vertical, and make it something you personally care about, then (2) go really, really deep in that vertical and don't worry if it pulls you away from this legal marketplace idea. It doesn't matter if it doesn't seem scalable at first. Just go really deep in that vertical and see where you come out."

So we floated two verticals by him on the spot and started brainstorming. Our first one was DUIs, since we figured there are a lot of young kids who get pulled over and don't want their parents to know. And it was a great fit because they could use our service anonymously and online, without telling their parents and without it costing much money. That may have been good in theory, but none of us had ever gotten a DUI before, and I still don't even have a driver's license, so there wasn't a personal connection with the problem.

Our next idea was immigration, and we certainly had a personal connection to that problem. I'm not a US citizen, and I've spent twenty-two of my now twenty-six years on a visa. Michael, my then cofounder, is Belgian, and was also on a visa at the time. We both found it incredibly difficult to stay on top of our own immigration paperwork. It's ironic, right? I'm a lawyer running this legal startup on a visa, and I find it hard to manage my own visa. That's weird. Maybe other people share this problem. And PG said, "Yeah, that seems like a good idea, because I was just talking to [a founder of a large technology company], and he was saying that even they spend tons of time project managing all this immigration nonsense. Do you want me to introduce you right now?" At that point, Michael and I asked ourselves, "All right, are we going to focus on immigration, or are we going to stay the course with the legal marketplace? And if we focus on immigration, what does that mean, and what do we do?"

In the end, we decided that if we were going to kill the legal marketplace to focus on immigration, we should be sure. We couldn't get any of the random visitors to our site to talk to us, so as a test we paid people off of Craigslist twenty dollars each to come to our office, sit with us, and go through our site. We ended up hiring fifteen people this way off of Craigslist. We told them, "Okay, let's pretend you're looking for a lawyer, and this is the website that somehow your friend has told you to go to. Tell us what you think." And, oh my God, the feedback was horrible. They basically all said, "Why the hell would I ever use this? I would probably just go to Yelp or ask a friend." It was just so bad and exactly what we should have done at the start. But after that very demoralizing day, we knew that if the legal marketplace idea wasn't dead before, it certainly was then. And we literally started from scratch the next day, throwing out the code base and starting over from scratch, knowing only that we were going to "fix immigration." Which was fun.

GUO: With your newfound knowledge, how did building and growing the new company compare to the old one?

RICHARDS: We basically did exactly the opposite of what we did with the legal marketplace. I don't think we even launched a public site until the day before Demo Day, because our first goal was to get a paying customer, paying us anything. Even a dollar, we would have taken it. Just any nonzero amount. So we emailed other founders we know asking if any of them wanted help with immigration stuff. And we got a lot of responses. Some people wanted to pay us for a project management tool for immigration. Other people asked us if we could just do visas for them. And doing someone's visa, that costs at least $3,000. I was like, "Oh wow, three grand up front, I'll happily take that over forty dollars a month for a Software as a Service product." So I literally did someone's visa, by hand. It's still unclear to me why he let me do it, but that was our first paying customer.

Soon afterwards it was Demo Day and I was fundraising, so we had to figure out where we wanted to go with the business. Clearly we had a business, because we made more money in one day than our legal marketplace made in one year, but we didn't know how to go from $3,000 to $30,000, and $30,000 to $300,000, and so on. The logical next step, which we did, was to just keep doing more and more visas for people. Even though our customers were small startups, a lot of startups have this problem. So we just did all their visas. And the fundraising story was that given enough time, we would either figure out a way to automate the process, so we'd be robots doing visas, or we'd build up a software tool into something sustainable that would, I don't know, maybe let us stop doing visas altogether.

Eventually, we came up with the idea of building a network. We thought, "Instead of us doing all the visas ourselves, let's get a network of lawyers to do the visas." And so that's how we launched our network of lawyers. Our first lawyer was a great immigration lawyer who had reached out to me over LinkedIn cold. I said, "Hey, you're an immigration lawyer, right? Would you like to do this visa for us? We'll pay you." And he agreed. So instead of us doing visa work for people, we started shipping it out to lawyers and charging a markup over their rates for our software and project management. And as it turns out, that's a pretty scalable business model. And it's just so ironic, because it's kind of like the legal marketplace idea come full circle, only this time with paying customers.

GUO: Did you go out of your way to communicate with these users or delight them?

RICHARDS: We once picked up two employees who we'd brought in on a visa for the same customer. They came on the same flight from France and we picked them up in a car, had hot towels and drinks ready for them, and then we took them straight to the Five Guys at SFO [San Francisco International Airport]. And we also got them beard warmers because we had heard they were really into SF hipster culture.

In general, though, it felt much more like a consulting job in the early days. So if a customer said they had a problem in any way related to hiring or managing expatriate employees, we would just offer a way to fix it, even if it had nothing to do with immigration. We still do this today. One customer, after getting a visa, also needed a nanny, since finding a nanny in Palo Alto is really hard and he was moving with a young family. So I found them a nanny agency.

Another time, a company told us that some of their employees felt as though their kids weren't going to good schools after relocating for work. And there's a problem that we could maybe one day solve, by having real estate brokers be part of our network the same way lawyers are. We're also looking pretty seriously at expanding into relocation by partnering with moving companies the same way we do with lawyers.

It seems to always work way better when you start with the customer and then figure it out from there, as opposed to building something out before you have the customer.

All of these things, you could call them doing things that don't scale. They're experiments, no different than Uber delivering ice cream or kittens on random days. You just see what works. And some of them are crazy, certainly none of them are scalable, but some of them work and you go from there. Take taxes. As it turns out, a lot of expats need help with taxes as well as immigration, side by side, because one affects the other. And we can help them with both because we already have all their data from their visa filing. To return to your question, one day, I think that delight will come from bundling it all; if we solve enough of these problems in one place, then it'll be a pretty delightful experience for the customer.

GUO: And how was the experience of growing beyond just small companies?

RICHARDS: It was surprisingly not terrible, because we just started talking to bigger and bigger customers, at which point there *is* a market for the immigration project management tool in addition to the visa work. So by going through investors, going through LinkedIn, going through whatever channel we could find, we hustled our way into getting [a large technology company] as our first enterprise reference customer. And they use us as a complete solution: a project management tool integrated with a network of lawyers who provide visas and advice. One day, we want to add additional services like tax and relocation, and additional countries, so that customers can use us to move their employees to, say, China, the same way that right now they currently use us to move and manage expatriate employees in the United States.

If we keep going, one day it will be this seamless experience to move people all over the world. But it all started with me doing a visa for somebody. And we still have a long way to go. We still manually do some parts of visas; in fact, there's a lot of work we do in-house that we just haven't figured out how to automate or send to our network yet, but that's fine—one day we will.

An example is the government forms for visas. They require wet-ink signatures, so you have to mail two-hundred-page documents out to get them physically signed, and the signatures have to be real wet ink. You can't e-sign them. And because our lawyers are somewhere in Texas, somewhere in Seattle, and our customers are in, say, Mountain View, we've had to FedEx these forms to Texas, get them back, FedEx them to Mountain View, get them back, and then FedEx them to the government. It's crazy, right? So we're working on an autopen machine and some custom printing solutions to see if we can do this better. If it works, we won't need to do FedEx anymore. And that saves us at least one hundred dollars and one week per visa.

So we always do things manually first, and then figure out ways to automate and scale it once we understand it, just like this autopen or our network of lawyers. It seems to always work way better when you start with the customer and then figure it out from there, as opposed to building something out before you have the customer.

CHAPTER 2: GENERAL ASSEMBLY

Brad Hargreaves, Cofounder

When you look at the landscape of programming-education companies today, there are dozens if not hundreds of options to choose from. There are free online coding lessons, intensive boot camps that last several weeks and cost thousands of dollars, and everything in between. Although General Assembly got its start as a shared working space, or coworking space, it quickly moved to the forefront of a group of companies intent on disrupting traditional education models.

General Assembly has been very intent on bridging the gap between universities and the rapidly changing demands of the market; today, the company offers workshops, online classes, and fully immersive programs for students. Over the last five years, the founders (Brad Hargreaves, Matt Brimer, Jake Schwartz, and Adam Pritzker) have learned an impressive amount about growing a company; General Assembly sits at the intersection of education and brick-and-mortar businesses, both of which are incredibly hard to build.

Strangely, most universities do a poor job of teaching industry best practices when it comes to software development. They maintain that they do not mold curriculum to the rapidly changing standards of the industry, but instead teach theoretical tenets like algorithms and systems programming. Whether this method is more effective than self-learning, paired with programs like General Assembly, remains to be seen.

GUO: How did you start working on this company?

HARGREAVES: So there are four of us who are cofounders, and we actually started thinking independently along similar lines. We wanted to create this community, this hub, for people in the technology and design world. Matt [Brimer] was probably the first one to say, "All right, we're going to build this thing; we're going to lease a space." I've known Matt since college; we started two businesses together in college, and he was the one who really rallied all of us together.

We had this vision that it would not only be a space where everybody could get together, but it would also have a big educational component as well. At the time, we didn't necessarily know what that meant. And we certainly didn't know that the core of the business was going to become education. But we really wanted to try creating a school from scratch. We started doing this by including a clause in the contract of every one of our coworking members that said they had to teach a class in the space.

They had to teach a class once a quarter, and we would split the revenue. That became the majority of our revenue pretty quickly, after we launched in January of 2011. And probably within four months of opening our doors, we realized that we weren't a coworking business—we were an education company. We always kind of knew that we wanted to be an education company, but by doing something that didn't scale, using our members as teachers, we were able to accelerate that process and find a business model that worked.

GUO: How did you find people to attend the classes?

HARGREAVES: In the very early days, we were aggressive about building our email list. We took our entire Gmail contact lists and dumped them into a MailChimp account, and we had six thousand people on our email list, just like that. We also collected emails from everyone who showed up to a meeting, which really helped accelerate the growth of the list.

I can't name a single innovative brick-and-mortar startup that wasn't running in some sort of gray area for some part of their existence. Or for their entire existence.

We were getting thirty to fifty new emails a day in the New York area. We really scraped it together on the email side and knew from the beginning that email marketing was how we were going to sell these courses. We bet on that one channel, and it worked out for us. Another thing that we did was run massive, massive hackathons in our space. We had a Foursquare hackathon; we had a hackathon on behalf of the New York City government; we had some crazy things.

The tough thing about running a business that involves physical space is that so many of the codes and the laws that govern physical space are so, so much stricter than things in virtual space. And you almost inevitably end up running in some kind of gray area. I can't name a single innovative brick-and-mortar startup that wasn't running in some sort of gray area for some part of their existence. Or for their entire existence. Look at Airbnb, look at Uber, look at all of these companies. It's very, very hard to do things in meatspace without being comfortable operating in a gray area.

GUO: What made you decide to pivot away from coworking and towards education?

HARGREAVES: One thing was we saw a bigger societal need on the education side. We were seeing a big disconnect with our peers who had graduated in the last ten years. Many of them were very well educated and had a lot of student debt, but didn't necessarily have the skills that matched the jobs that were available in the marketplace. All of the companies that were working out of the coworking space needed to hire a web developer, and user experience designers, and digital marketers, and product managers. And there wasn't anyone coming out of university that knew these skills in the way that these companies wanted them to.

There are some relatively minor gaps, like the gap between being a web developer and being a computer science major, but there are also some serious macro issues. Even if you ignore the smaller issues, there's a massive deficit in the number of computer science majors coming out of college versus the number of available jobs and the demand for people who have that skill set in the market. So we said, "There's actually going to be a huge societal need for a different kind of educational company that is lighter." We wanted something that didn't have the same fixed-cost structure that a traditional university has and therefore didn't have to charge as much money. And something that's a lot more flexible, that didn't operate on a semester system but instead had rolling admission throughout the year.

GUO: After the pivot, how did you recruit teachers?

HARGREAVES: Well, it was all very informal in the early days. As long as they stuck within the general guidelines, teachers could teach whatever they wanted to teach, however they wanted to teach it. And in the early days we really struck the right balance there, because if we had gone in either direction—being too prescriptive or too laissez-faire—I think we would have run into problems.

For instance, because the teachers could experiment with what they wanted to teach, within some bounds, we were able to discover which topics sold well and which didn't. We knew

---

I think one of the reasons General Assembly succeeded where other similar models failed was that we did constrain the [course] topics. . . . As much as we wanted to be scrappy and, you know, laissez-faire about this stuff, I think it was very, very important that we did set those boundaries and define who we were really early on.

---

where there was a lot of demand. We had one teacher who taught a programming for nonprogrammers workshop. We had some concerns about the class being too high level, but it sold *incredibly* well. The students loved it, and they got a lot out of it, even if the outcome was "become more fluent in the art of programming" instead of "become a programmer."

So the fact that we let instructors experiment was a very positive thing. On the other hand, I think one of the reasons General

Assembly succeeded where other similar models failed was that we did constrain the topics. So if you wanted to teach broadly in the topics of online marketing, web development, design, entrepreneurship, you could teach really anything in those topic areas. But if you wanted to come and teach cooking, or teach a foreign language, or teach a pickup artistry class, then Skillshare was probably a better fit. That's not what we do at General Assembly, and I think being able to articulate that identity was incredibly important. As much as we wanted to be scrappy and, you know, laissez-faire about this stuff, I think it was very, very important that we did set those boundaries and define who we were really early on.

We also found that different people have different motivations. A lot of what we really struggled to understand early on was what motivates someone to teach. Some people want to teach because they make money by teaching. So however many hundreds of dollars they were getting for teaching for an evening actually made it worth their time. Other people want to teach because they love interacting with students and they really want to transfer their knowledge and they enjoy teaching. Other people want to teach because they want to put it on their resume and point at it later.

There's nothing wrong with these, and I try not to make value judgments. We don't think, "Well, it's better to teach because you like teaching and that's the only good reason to teach." If we did believe that, we would have a lot harder time finding teachers. You have to understand why each person is teaching and be able to speak to that desire. So if you go to a successful founder and say, "Hey, come here and teach for the evening, here's $200," they're going to be borderline insulted. If it's much more about connecting with people and transferring their knowledge, you can explain that maybe they'll meet some awesome people in the audience that could become their next generation of interns or employees.

And that's a much more valuable proposition. You really have to understand what drives people, on a person-by-person basis, and put an offer together that is going to motivate them.

GUO: Describe the experience of expanding to new cities.

HARGREAVES: So the model of, you know, "we'll just open up, and let anyone teach anything for a short period of time within some constraints," that didn't scale. You *can't* scale that by just making it bigger and doing it on a bigger scale. The way you scale up an education business is actually by making the value proposition for the student more transformative.

We did this by saying, "We know there's an interest in web development, we know there's an interest in design, we know there's an interest in digital marketing, so rather than offering more hour-long evening digital marketing classes, we are going to create a ten-week-long digital marketing course, and offer that in a more productized way at a higher price point." And we wanted to speak to what a student will be able to do in their job after they've gone through that course.

I would even say the next level of scale above that is to look at user-experience design or web development, and ask the question, "What would a student have to learn to get themselves a job as a web developer?" And that's really how we scaled the education model: not by taking the scrappy thing we were doing originally and doing more of it, but by actually taking the indications we were getting about the value propositions that resonated and really delivering on those value propositions.

And I think that was a conclusion that came out of a lot of research about what's happening in education. We didn't do a lot of research about education and come in with a deep-seated thesis when we just started running these classes. We only did that research after the classes started working. And then we asked the question of "How do you scale this?" Because we really had an audience, we knew we were onto something, but we didn't know what we were onto. I think the lesson that came out of that, for us, was that you have to ask the hard questions of "Why is this working?" and "What is the right direction to go next?" rather than blindly following the path you're already on.

[Sometimes] scale is a weasel word. It's a weasel word people use to avoid having to think hard about hard problems. They end up going and building photo-sharing apps because that's what sells, rather than tackling hard, meaningful, interesting social problems.

Another lesson that we've learned is that it's all about the people. The markets that have worked for us are the markets where we've been able to put a leader on the ground who can represent General Assembly's values. It's typically someone who has seen other General Assemblies and someone who knows how to manage people and how to represent the brand. So the basic challenge is finding those great, talented people who can be leaders and run a campus with no other supervision on the ground—run a campus that delivers on the value proposition.

GUO: What's one thing that you've learned about scaling this business so far?

HARGREAVES: Well, one thing I think about a lot is how do you define scalable versus unscalable? That is, what does it mean for something to scale? You can look at brick-and-mortar stores, which have to deal with half a million square feet of space, with butts in seats, and think they're unscalable. But there are *massive* businesses, companies like Shake Shack or Chipotle, that are running hard-core brick-and-mortar operations in meatspace. I think a lot of people throw around words like *scalable* or *unscalable* without thinking deeper about what that means.

Personally, I like bringing the definition back to dollars, and thinking about operating leverage, where each marginal dollar of revenue that you get is not as costly as the last dollar of revenue. So with $100 million in annual revenue, your operating margins are better than they were at $50 million in annual revenue. And if you're at $250 million in annual revenue, it will be even better still. Does that make sense?

Because otherwise *scale* is a weasel word. It's a weasel word people use to avoid having to think hard about hard problems. They end up going and building photo-sharing apps because that's what sells, rather than tackling hard, meaningful, interesting social problems like education, or real estate, or health care, because they don't "scale." And I think a lot of people have embraced the intellectual laziness of dismissing some types of innovation and some types of industries by just saying they don't scale, when in fact what they mean is that they're complicated and they're hard.

CHAPTER 3: CROWDBOOSTER

Ricky Yean, Cofounder & CEO

In the summer of 2006, a then-unknown site launched with the name "Twttr." Four years later, the company was barely recognizable; it had changed its name to Twitter, its users sent over fifty million tweets per day, and it had helped spawn an entire wave of companies dedicated to understanding and managing this new "social media" trend. One of those companies was Crowdbooster.

Crowdbooster offers tools to help users improve their online presence via analytics; once you connect your social media accounts, you can monitor and boost several metrics. The company was founded in 2010 by Ricky Yean, David Tran, and Mark Linsey and entered a market with strong competition.

Nevertheless, the founders persevered, and they were able to recruit celebrities like Britney Spears, Tim Ferriss, and Ashton Kutcher to the platform, often breaking things along the way. In refining their product over so many years, it's interesting to note that the founders experimented with ideas that would become companies in and of themselves. Navigating the maze of successful startup concepts is never easy, and Yean remarks, "If you're smart enough to dig deeper, you might notice opportunities right in front of you that people are dying to solve."

GUO: How did you meet your Crowdbooster cofounders? How did you get your idea?

YEAN: David and I were working together as part of a student organization at Stanford called BASES. We weren't friends before, but we wanted to join BASES because we both were interested in entrepreneurship, and we ended up having complementary skill sets. And when we first started working together, we really liked each other. From that point on, we decided that outside of BASES we should do stuff together.

We got into Y Combinator after applying to it for the second time. When we applied, we had been working together for about a year on various products, and the product that got us accepted at the time was actually something that wasn't Crowdbooster. Once we were in YC—this is before they had significant investment money—we only had $20K. We knew that we didn't have enough money to keep going for much longer after Demo Day if we didn't raise money, so we were definitely feeling some pressure.

We explored various ideas and built prototypes during those twelve weeks, but by the time we had six weeks left, we hadn't settled on a product. We thought we didn't have enough money and needed to start making some. We were obsessed with social media in general, so we thought, "Hey, why not do consulting for social media for small businesses and get paid for it? And build out internal tools simultaneously?" Then we walked down University Avenue [in Palo Alto] and went into every store and asked them if they had a Twitter page and if they needed someone to help them manage it. Most of them didn't [have Twitter], and the ones who did didn't care about it.

We didn't get any traction until we walked into Coupa Café and met the owner, this tech-savvy guy who also went to Stanford. Immediately he said, "Yes, I want somebody to help me with social media stuff because I don't know anything about it." Then we asked him to pay us for it. He hesitated, and then decided to pay us in food instead.

I emailed and I asked, "Who are you going to use our product for? What account are we going to be putting into our system?" And she said, "Britney Spears." And we said, "Holy shit."

So me, David, and Mark, the three of us, basically moved into the back of Coupa in downtown Palo Alto. We took all our meetings there. We had all three meals there and three coffees in between. We had this table in the back which was our go-to. I was the nontechnical person, so I'd be the one doing all the tweeting and coming up with interesting things to say about coffee and trying to get people to come in the door, and the other guys would build tools to help me.

In order to keep the free food coming, we had to make reports to the Coupa guy, so we started building this dashboard, and then polishing up the dashboard that we had built, and then adding more metrics, and that's how the first version of Crowdbooster came to be. Once we had Coupa, we started asking other people to use it. We were able to get two hundred users by Demo Day. All that happened in six weeks.

GUO: Before you built what became Crowdbooster, why did you pivot away from your earlier ideas?

YEAN: At the time, we really didn't know what we were doing. We had built many more products before Crowdbooster, but we had one that we spent maybe six months on. We had some users, maybe fifty or so. They weren't what we envisioned. They came from random places on the Internet, and so we didn't really pay much attention to them. We didn't really know where to take it.

I think we pivoted mainly because we weren't willing to do things like really try to figure out why people were using it, if they were using it at all. In general, not that many people were using it, so I don't know how much we could have gotten from talking to them.

GUO: How did you get your first hundred or so Crowdbooster users?

YEAN: In the beginning, we had this analytics dashboard where you would connect your Twitter and see all the metrics, but we had a few other tools too. Like we would help you automatically follow people on Twitter, which was kind of spammy, but it was actually quite useful. You automatically follow people and then wait till they follow you back, and if they don't follow you back, you can drop them. So it was really a great way to build up your follower account at that point.

That was how we made Follow Builder, which we don't offer as a product anymore. We shut it down three years ago, but for our first few thousand users, that feature was quite useful. We never thought it was sustainable, because it was kind of scammy, but it did help us acquire the first thousand or ten thousand users, because that was one of the key features that they wanted. Later on, people built similar products that made it onto TechCrunch and Hacker News, but Twitter eventually shut them all down. We built that back in 2010 or '11.

The way we approached people, we obviously used Twitter, and we would message everyone on Twitter. We had a page where we would search for all kinds of variations of *Twitter* and *analytics*, and then we would just message people when they were complaining about it or asking about it, to get them to try our product. That was one way.

Another was, I was spending a lot of time on Quora, and at that time the only thing that we were thinking about is getting users. So I naturally searched for Twitter analytics questions on Quora, and then I saw a comment to an answer to a question related to Twitter analytics. The comment was like, "This tool X doesn't really work that well. Does anyone else know another one?" So I directly messaged that person when I saw the comment and she said, "Oh yeah, sure. I would love to learn more about your product; you can find my email at this URL."

Then I went to the URL, which was her website, and it claimed she was a Hollywood manager, among other things. I emailed and I asked, "Who are you going to use our product for? What account are we going to be putting into our system?" And she said, "Britney Spears." And we said, "Holy shit." It was nuts. Our system literally could not handle it at the time; it was a prototype.

So Britney Spears just signed up as one of the two hundred users in the beginning. And she broke our site multiple, multiple times. But fortunately her manager had her credentials, so she could always just reauthenticate with us to fix it.

I would read Mashable a lot because Mashable wrote a lot about social media. Once, the site had an article about Lil Wayne and how Lil Wayne was one of the biggest celebrities on social media. He was very savvy on Twitter and Facebook. Then at the end of the article, it had the name of Lil Wayne's manager. So I tracked down the manager's email and I messaged him.

As it turns out, that guy is four years younger than me, and we could speak on the same level because we're the same age. Well, not the same age, but we're close enough that we immediately hit it off. We got him to put Lil Wayne in there and he put in some of Lil Wayne's label, so Drake, Nicki Minaj, like those guys. He had access to all those guys.

Every one of these stories sounds like luck, but for every fifty emails that I send to somebody's manager, one of them will reply. So constantly thinking about it, and constantly doing something about it, is how you hit the jackpot once in a while.

Once, [Mashable] had an article about Lil Wayne and how Lil Wayne was one of the biggest celebrities on social media. He was very savvy on Twitter and Facebook. Then at the end of the article, it had the name of Lil Wayne's manager. So I tracked down the manager's email and I messaged him.

GUO: How did you deal with the times when your site broke?

YEAN: We had to do a lot of things to try to patch it. Eventually we rewrote the entire thing for scale, but before that we had to just manually fix everything, which was not fun. We also worked to hold on to the relationship with Britney Spears's manager; we drove down to LA to meet her, so she could put a face to the company. It wasn't an important discussion; it was mostly to get to know them and help develop the relationship.

The same thing happened when one of Britney Spears's good friends, Ashton Kutcher, told us that he wanted to meet with us. Again, we went and drove down to LA to meet with Ashton, and he signed up right away. We grabbed these opportunities, one after another. We didn't really question them. I think at the time we were just so happy that it was so different from before, that people actually wanted to use our stuff.

GUO: In what other ways did you go the extra mile for your early users?

YEAN: In the beginning, you do all your [own] support. You email people to ask them how they are doing. You call them up. If they're nearby, you visit them and buy them coffee or lunch. So that sort of became a regular thing. Nothing really crazy happened as a result, but because it had worked for us before, it became part of the culture of the company to keep doing that.

It's also rewarding. Even when the rewards diminish over time because each user is just a smaller deal over time, the appreciation has been built up as part of the company culture, and that's how we do it.

Another person who we did things for was Tim Ferriss. One of the features that we had showed you who your biggest followers were on Twitter. So once Tim Ferriss got connected to us and signed up for the platform, we started talking to him about his book launch. He was launching *The 4-Hour Body*, I think, and he wanted to send advance copies to the big Twitter influencers that were already following him.

He asked us if we could give him a list of people like that. Our platform had the top fifty, but he wanted the top thousand, which was relatively easy for us to do, but it still required work that we weren't getting paid for. Although Tim Ferriss tweeted about it, which probably drove more users.

We did some of these things for Britney too. Aside from just using our platform, she wanted some custom features. Britney Spears was on *American Idol* as one of the judges, and "she" was tweeting alongside the show while the show aired live. The show was live, and her team was also tweeting live. What they wanted to show was that when Britney tweeted live, engagement went through the roof.

For example, #AmericanIdol: compare people who are talking about #AmericanIdol to people who are talking about #AmericanIdol and #BritneySpears or @BritneySpears—how much did Britney increase the level of conversation and how much of the conversation was because of Britney? They were trying to show Britney's influence on TV.

These were the very early days of Twitter with TV. Twitter kind of knew that TV was a big deal, but they hadn't done much about it. We did an analysis for them, and we put together really good reports that they used to show Fox or someone. All those things were not part of the product, and we had to do extra work for it. We did it once or twice, and that really cemented the relationship.

> *We asked [the owner of Coupa Café] to pay us for [Crowdbooster]. He hesitated, and then decided to pay us in food instead.*

Thinking about it, later on, there were multiple products that did this. Twitter bought this company called BlueFin Technologies, or something similar, that basically analyzed Twitter's impact on TV. Twitter bought it for tens of millions of dollars because Twitter has an advertising product that is sold to TV stations and they need metrics around that. So Twitter invested in basically Twitter plus TV companies.

We didn't really explore the opportunity, but one reason why you should consider these unscalable things is because if you're smart enough to dig deeper, you might notice opportunities right in front of you that people are dying to solve. By doing these unscalable things, you might put yourself in the position to notice those things. Obviously, you have to understand what is going on in the industry. Maybe we didn't really have a good understanding of the potential there, but if we did, we might have been able to seize on that opportunity early on. So who knows?

One reason why you should consider these unscalable things is because if you're smart enough to dig deeper, you might notice opportunities right in front of you that people are dying to solve.

GUO: How easy was it to transition the custom work into the main product?

YEAN: Honestly, we didn't do much of that. But working on it definitely taught us things. For example, it taught us what a large account looks like and feels like and what it does to our system. So with that experience we were able to build something that was able to scale to hundreds of thousands of users with no problem. I think that experience was helpful.

Something that did make it back into the core product was reporting. We needed to show reports to Coupa Café, and I was cobbling the reports together in Word and PowerPoint. I would use different free tools, take screenshots of the outputs, and paste the results in. One of the key features that we have now is the ability to show you who's following you, not just as a number but who the person is. It tells a story about who these thousands of your followers are.

We figured out that with social media, which is not closely tied to the bottom line, a huge emphasis is placed on storytelling and anecdotes. If you can say, "Hey, we added one thousand followers," that's meaningless to the business. That doesn't mean anything businesswise because you can't sell more things with that information. With most marketing—awareness types of marketing—that's always true. So the way you overcome that is by saying, "We have one thousand followers; one of them is Paul Graham and the other is Dave McClure." So I was looking for interesting followers on our list, and we decided to build a feature for that, and now that's still a really popular feature.

A lot of these things kind of give you an understanding of why certain features are useful. When you build a product, you might be one step removed from the actual user experience, but when you're doing the unscalable thing of trying to be the user or trying very hard to sell and acquire the user, then you get an additional level of understanding. You understand it; you can feel it in your skin, a feeling like "this needs to exist."

CHAPTER 4: FLIGHTCAR

Rujul Zaparde, Cofounder & CEO

FlightCar is a marketplace that lets people rent their cars out while they're traveling. Buyers get cars at a fraction of airport rental prices, and sellers get money they wouldn't have made otherwise. The company came at a time when the sharing economy was taking off; Airbnb had been around for nearly seven years, and companies like RelayRides (car sharing) and 99dresses (clothing sharing) were establishing footholds as well.

A common mantra among startups is "Ask for forgiveness, not permission," and FlightCar is certainly an embodiment of this mantra; the company is currently being sued by the city of San Francisco. The city maintains that FlightCar is competing with car rental companies but is ignoring the regulations that govern them.

Conflicts like these are increasingly common; startups are sidestepping regulations in their eagerness to disrupt existing markets, and governments are struggling to play catch-up. Airbnb has faced numerous lawsuits regarding hotel regulations, and Uber and Lyft have repeatedly been sued in their battle with the taxi industry. This balance is a delicate one; incumbents can and often do abuse their power to stifle progress and dominate upstarts, but it is important to remember that many of these regulations were initially created to protect consumers.

The company was founded by Rujul Zaparde, Kevin Petrovic, and Shri Ganeshram in 2012. When the company was founded, all three were between seventeen and eighteen years old, having deferred admission to college in order to pursue the startup dream.

GUO: How did you meet your FlightCar cofounders?

ZAPARDE: Back in February 2012 I read an article on Airbnb about how people were sharing their houses with others. And that was the first time I'd heard about Airbnb. I grew up in Jersey, right near Princeton, and the day after I read that article I met with my now-cofounder Kevin, and we started talking about ideas.

We were just talking out loud, and we said, "If your most valuable asset is your house, then your second most valuable asset is your car." Kevin has done a bunch of traveling, so we put two and two together and started talking about airports. That's the only place where people will pay money to have their car sit there and do nothing, and next door you have thousands of Hertz-owned cars that are rented out at fifty to sixty dollars a day. And the inefficiency couldn't be any more blatant there.

So that's how we came up with the idea. We didn't think we'd start a company out of it, initially. We spent a couple of months doing car rental searches, among other things. We got a feel for the market, and we reached the point of "Okay, let's start a company around this." We ended up going through two startup accelerators: the Brandery from July to October of 2012, but we knew we wanted to launch in San Francisco, so we went through

Y Combinator from January to March of 2013. And in February of 2013 we launched our first-ever rental. We raised a couple of rounds after that, and right now we're in nine cities.

GUO: What made you decide to pull the trigger on the company?

ZAPARDE: I would say curiosity. It was a really cool idea, and we were genuinely curious as to whether people would actually use the service and if we could pull off turning it into a business. It was definitely a challenge, and it would have been too interesting to *not* try. So at that point we incorporated, and went at it.

When we first started, I would drive to the airport at four o'clock in the morning in order to take people's keys. . . . I would hand-wash a lot of the cars—I vacuumed hundreds of cars—in the first couple of months.

GUO: After incorporation, how did you start collecting users?

ZAPARDE: Right, so that's when we launched. I remember we first went live at one a.m., the middle of the night, and basically nothing happened. It took around two weeks for the first rental to happen, with us feeding inventory into the system a little bit.

We were essentially getting cars from other sources, so we'd lease cars and rent them out again in the system. So in the system you'd see "Rujul's Honda Accord," which would be the car we leased, and it would show us as the owners. We started it off like that, and it took us about two or three weeks until the first person who actually listed their own car, and we actually clicked and rented that other person's car. That was our first actual transaction with somebody else's car.

Our model actually worked really well for a marketplace, given that most marketplaces have to solve the chicken-and-egg problem when they get started. We seeded the inventory a little bit at first, but as people starting using the service, every car that got rented meant another car somewhere else became available.

When we first started, I would drive to the airport at four o'clock in the morning in order to take people's keys. We would give you the car, and I'd be there in a green FlightCar vest, a uniform. I would hand-wash a lot of the cars—I vacuumed hundreds of cars—in the first couple of months. We basically did everything ourselves, and we delayed hiring additional employees for at least the first month or two, because we *wanted* to do it ourselves. We learned a lot from it, and now I know all sorts of stuff like how to properly dry a car without leaving water spots, things like that.

We did that because it was the type of business where we were active 24-7, 365. We would take support calls all the time; we would have a system where it would ring one person's phone, then ring the second person's phone, and so on. Whoever had night duty, their phone would ring and the other two guys would be really pissed if he didn't pick up the call. So we did that for almost three or four months. We got to the point where whoever was on duty couldn't really sleep, because there were at least twenty calls coming in during the night.

Now, our system is good enough to automatically figure out the most efficient match if you rent a car. If you rent a sedan, it'll figure out that "John's Camry" is available at the right time, and assign it to you automatically. Before that, we had to manage everything on a spreadsheet. We did that for three or four months, up to the point where we had seventy, eighty cars all being tracked on a Google Docs spreadsheet.

Every night we had to allocate the cars, which meant figuring out who was getting which car, and doing it as efficiently as possible, which took about four hours per day. Because allocating one car affects the other inventory, and if you don't allocate as efficiently as possible you can run out of cars much faster. And that was how a lot of things worked back then, on spreadsheets. We even had a ton of things that were paper based, like Hertz, where we had carbon copies of things, although nowadays things are paperless.

Took us a while to get there, and when we started out it was just two cofounders, and we basically did everything. Nowadays, as you might imagine, we have a lot of hourly employees because we have to wash the cars and all sorts of other stuff. We're probably around a hundred people right now, but maybe seventy-five of them are hourly employees.

GUO: Walk me through the process of listing a car back then.

ZAPARDE: So when someone listed their car, it wouldn't show up on the website automatically. We would receive an email about the car, and one of us would have to go and manually create a listing in the system. When you rented somebody's car, all it did was charge your card via Stripe, and it would email support@flightcar.com saying, "John has rented a car." That was it. And I would take that email, manually star it in the in-box, and transcribe it into the spreadsheet. The customers never saw all this, of course, but it was extremely manual on the back end.

And I remember when this process started to really break down. During the Fourth of July weekend in 2013, we had serious issues. We had way more reservations than we had ever had at that point. Even though we dwarf those numbers now, back then it was a lot for us, especially with our lack of systems. And I remember that crazy weekend because we worked about thirty hours straight, just to make sure everything was working for our customers. With the allocations, I had twice as many problems; it took around seven or eight hours to figure out the car distribution. That was when it started breaking down.

The good news is that our first automated system went live around July 7, three days later. Obviously we've changed it a lot since then to automate things even further, but it was what we needed at the time.

We were essentially getting cars from other sources, so we'd lease cars and rent them out again in the system. So in the system you'd see "Rujul's Honda Accord," which would be the car we leased, and it would show us as the owners.

GUO: Has the overall transition away from manual processes been smooth?

ZAPARDE: Obviously right now things go a lot smoother than back then, but with any transition, there are always going to be hiccups. You just have to wait until the hiccup happens and solve that problem. Every system is meant to deal with certain things, but when the volume of those things goes beyond what's normal, then some aspects of the system are going to break down.

With us, our system handled airport pickups for a while, early on. You'd call in, and we'd manually call the limo driver. Now, each limo driver has an app on their phone, and they get a pickup request with a location, and things go much more smoothly. But that took time; first there was a basic app, but people would still have to call; then there was a web app available, but we had to take things step by step. There were times—like over Christmas, when we had 150 different parties getting picked up at the same time—when certain parts of that app didn't work very well, so we had to make some changes. But things are always going to break down with enough volume. I don't know if you can ever make it 100 percent perfect.

GUO: Since then, has user growth been manual or organic?

ZAPARDE: It has mostly been organic growth, especially on the parking side. With the renters' side, we tried a lot of things early on, like AdWords. There was a day where my cofounder and I wore our FlightCar uniforms, a green vest with our logo on it, and we stood next to a busy intersection that was near an airport. We stood there for ten or twelve hours, and we had a giant banner that said, "Ask us about free airport parking."

During the Fourth of July weekend in 2013, we had serious issues. We had way more reservations than we had ever had at that point. . . . And I remember that crazy weekend because we worked about thirty hours straight, just to make sure everything was working for our customers.

People really didn't like that, because you had to pass that intersection to get to one of the bigger paid airport parking lots. We had the police called on us at least three times that day. Fortunately I had called the police department in advance, and they told me I could stand there, since it was a public sidewalk. And each time the cops said, "It's a bit odd, but it's within their rights," so they were very cool about it.

Either way it didn't work out super well; we were two Indian kids standing on the sidewalk holding a sign, and we looked like idiots. Maybe it created some awareness, but nobody stopped to talk to us during those twelve hours.

GUO: Did you go above and beyond for your earliest users?

ZAPARDE: Yeah, obviously we were very responsive—we still are—to any complaints that we received. We would do whatever it took to make things right. One customer unfortunately had a bad experience, and I ended up offering to take him out to coffee, to get his feedback and to try and make up for it. Even though the drive took three hours, I spent my Saturday doing it to make sure I did everything I could.

And again, I still think we strive to make things right, but I'm not able to do things myself. Things like meeting customers and introducing myself as the founder, or showing up at two thirty in the morning to help a customer who's about to miss his flight, or taking people's cars to get broken taillights fixed, that sort of stuff. I do still respond to every single feedback email that comes in, and I still read every single customer survey.

CHAPTER 5: TILT

James Beshara, Cofounder & CEO

Like other companies in this book, Tilt (formerly Crowdtilt) is a company born out of the widespread adoption of a new technology. The current crowdfunding landscape was pioneered a few years before Tilt, in the form of crowdfunding giants Kickstarter (founded in 2009) and Indiegogo (founded in 2008). As those companies paved the way for novel uses of crowdfunding, companies like Tilt arose to meet market demands. (Interestingly, Tilt began as a site to give charitable donations, much like Watsi.)

Today, Tilt lets groups raise money online for any purpose. Founded in 2012 by James Beshara and Khaled Hussein, Tilt is the second approach to crowdfunding by Beshara (he previously founded the nonprofit crowdfunding site Dvelo.org).

One of the major lessons that Beshara has learned is that it is much more important to focus on trends rather than absolute numbers. Adding a thousand users every week sounds great until it's compared to 10 percent week-over-week growth; when you look at both graphs, the former actually has a *decreasing* growth rate. Human beings are generally bad at internalizing exponential growth curves, and one of the reasons why focusing on trends is important is that it allows you to track exponential growth without having to think too hard about the overall curve.

GUO: Tell me about the origins of Tilt.

BESHARA: Before Tilt, I built a crowdfunding startup called Dvelo.org, which focused on poverty alleviation. My background is in development economics, and I picked up web development in college on the side. My first startup was meant for people to collaborate and donate with their friends and family to international development organizations, specifically microfinance and microinsurance. Total mouthful, I know.

At the same time as I was building this out, the United States Securities and Exchange Commission changed their stance on online lending. Their new regulation ultimately killed our business model, but we learned a lot about how expensive it can be to operate in heavily regulated spaces. I think the biggest insight from the experience was that this little crowdfunding feature in the site that allowed you to invite friends and family to fund a loan together could be a lot bigger than my narrow, inflexible application of it. Basically, I had my own idea of how people should use this new kind of tool and didn't allow for much flexibility.

With Tilt, it was really important to me that the technology wasn't only built for a user that existed in my head but was flexible enough to learn from actual customers. And I flexed and bent the product around the people that found the most use in it. From the early days of Tilt until now, we never decided, "This is our customer, and this is our solution for them." It was more along the lines of "Let's build out something that looks a little bit like a solution, only so that we can get the earliest customer feedback to know what we should *actually* be building."

It sounds simple, but I think it's actually quite hard to balance the hubris and confidence that can go into carving your own path and starting a company with the mentality of "We're going to be wrong in a lot of ways, so wrong that let's just get something out the door as quickly as possible to see how wrong we are." The confidence, and honestly the hubris too, is extremely important, but so is the flexibility and understanding that no one—literally, no one—is right the first time. So just err on being wrong fast.

Thinking about it now, I'm sure I heard this advice during my first startup, but the sting of building something in a rigid way, working on it for seventeen months, then launching it and feeling the pain of being wrong really singed that self-awareness in my brain.

It was really important to me that the technology wasn't only built for a user that existed in my head but was flexible enough to learn from actual customers.

We were very open and flexible with how Tilt was used in the early days. Though we thought nonprofits were a good candidate for the narrow, edge-of-the-wedge way to get started, I had a friend who asked to use Tilt for a fantasy football league, a tailgate, and then a birthday party, and it was literally those three things that started to seed this marginal growth of other friends wanting to use it for all sorts of other similar things—a group trip, their kickball league, a wedding gift.

Seeing those campaigns lead to others splitting off, I thought, "Okay, that is where there is a market need, and there's more of a need right now than nonprofits and social fundraising software."

GUO: What was it like growing the site beyond the first dozen users?

BESHARA: We got to the first fifty users going through friends. It wasn't easy, as I would have dinners with someone to convince them to use it. Or I would schedule meetings with nonprofits. My cofounder, Khaled, and I would have conversations with anyone and everyone who would listen to us, and then watch them use the site closely to see if it was of any use to them.

The next growth phase, going from a hundred customers to a thousand, was an education in the realities of building a company with a massive user base. Every single company that gets to a crazy, critical mass of users, whether it's five hundred thousand users, or a million, or ten million users, they all have two things early on. They have a fraction of that critical mass, but they also have an amazing trend line. Back then, I thought maybe you launch something, and next comes ten thousand users—as if they're two singular points. If your product is *really* awesome, it'll get to a hundred thousand users. That's how these giant companies want to spin the story, but it's almost never the case. The reality is that they all sit there at fifty customers and work hard on their growth-trend line. They wallow at six hundred users trying to engineer a better trend line. I remember hearing that the first six months of Twitter's growth was relatively flat, or the first year of Snapchat was flat, and it made it clear that every company struggles with this.

It's a subtle refocusing from the vanity metrics that the press focuses on and shifts your mind-set to manage for process and not manage for result. If you nail the process and a healthy trend line, the results will take care of themselves. You can apply this to competitors or tangential opportunities too—it's not the number that matters; it's the trend. Week over week, month over month.

GUO: Has there been anything surprising about your growth so far?

BESHARA: Learning the power of growing 10 percent week over week really simplified it for us. It had nothing to do with focusing on those big numbers. It had everything to do with focusing on trends.

Every single company that gets to a crazy, critical mass of users, whether it's five hundred thousand users, or a million, or ten million users, they all have two things early on. They have a fraction of that critical mass, but they also have an amazing trend line.

GUO: With your earliest users, did you go above and beyond in your customer service?

BESHARA: We did everything. We sent handwritten notes to the first few thousand users. We sent Starbucks gift cards when we screwed up. We sent T-shirts to the first power users. The old convention of it being cheaper to retain a current customer rather than acquire a new one drove a lot of this. It was also unexpected for people to use software and get a human touch with the people that built the software. I think this is standard procedure now for most startups, but it was indicative of a larger theme of "do whatever it takes." We moved to four cities, rebuilt the site multiple times, have worked six- or seven-day weeks for the last three-plus years, wanted to rise above the noise of other startups to make an impression in people's minds, and truly loved our customers with every sense of the phrase, because we're committed to doing whatever it takes to make sure what we're building today has lasting, durable value seven, seventeen, and thirty years from now.

GUO: Were there any other lessons learned from sending handwritten notes or other delightful exercises?

BESHARA: For the first six or eight months, my cofounder and I knew what to build because I was talking directly to the users every day. At twenty-five people, you can easily get disconnected from the front lines of your customers, your users. And when that happens, you're disconnected from how they're using the product, where they're having pain points, and how to make the best product possible.

We got around that disconnect by recognizing that even at twenty-five, fifty, or seventy people, we're going to continue our tradition of everyone in the company doing customer support. Right now, we're at seventy people, and every one of us does customer support so that early dedication to our customers continues. Our director of product and one of our other best product managers, in fact, both started in customer support. Last year, when we started outlining our core values, the first one we defined was "Love Our Customers."

We're building this product for users that are not numbers on a graph but rather humans that have an issue with X on Tuesday, or Y on Friday. That's our viewpoint. It doesn't hurt that my friends still text me constantly about fixing this or adding in that.

GUO: What are your thoughts on scalability moving forward?

BESHARA: Every few months you've got to reassess how you're managing your resources. Because things that make sense at a certain size might not make sense down the road. It's much better to realize that you're doing things that don't scale, with a lot of people who love your product, instead of thinking that because certain things won't scale beyond a small number of users, that they're not worth doing in the first place.

The costs of starting these businesses is plummeting, but the costs of *building* these businesses is skyrocketing. The fact that anyone with $20,000 and a laptop can launch an application from a coffee shop in Kansas City, or Beijing, or London, means that building a viable business that rises above the noise of all the start-ups and products that launch every day—it's never been harder.

We internalized the first part of that—it's never been cheaper to start these businesses. And we realized starting it, and then building it, is like buying something and then figuring out the price later. You bought it, you started the company, you launched the application to the world. Now, the real price you pay is that you've got to grow it and build a business, not just an app.

The problem is, when you focus on what other companies did to build long-term, sustainable businesses, more often than not the only public evidence you can find is a *Wired* or *Fortune* article talking about them hitting a million users, then fifteen million users, then one hundred million users. So you understand that the hard part isn't launching; it's making sure enough people know that this company exists that you can hit a million users, and then fifteen million users. But I think when you do that analysis, and you see those public articles, you miss important opportunities.

In general, the phrase *achieve scale* is funny. Scale isn't something you achieve. It's not a destination; it's an input. Or something you add when things are working. It's much harder and much more important to find what's working and then figure out how to add scale afterward.

The whole premise behind "do things that don't scale" from Y Combinator is paradoxically that most founders and people are surprised by what they actually can scale. Just "do," and then you realize, if you're smart, you can figure out a way to scale what you're doing. Writing handwritten notes is providing a human touch that has the effect of delighting people. You can do that with witty copy or a video from the CEO to the super power users sent straight to their in-box. Exceeding customer expectations is scalable.

The costs of starting these businesses is plummeting, but the costs of building these businesses is skyrocketing. The fact that anyone with $20,000 and a laptop can launch an application from a coffee shop in Kansas City, or Beijing, or London, means that building a viable business that rises above the noise of all the startups and products that launch every day—it's never been harder.

To give it a more internal perspective, we really value overcommunication at Tilt. The effect is clarity and purpose in what you're doing, why you're doing it, and clear communication of your current and future value you bring to the team. The same clarity at five people is scalable at eight hundred people. Along the way, of course, you have to flush the system of the tactics, or process, that worked before—but you can scale clarity and purpose for team members through thousands of people if you're smart. But the way to relegate it a moot point is to think *scale* is an important box to check before you've found what works. It's just an input along the way, and if you're smart enough to find something that is working, then trust yourself to be smart enough to find a way to scale it.

CHAPTER 6: VERBLING

Jake Jolis, Cofounder & CEO

There is a fantastic diagram (originally attributed to Paul Graham and the partners at Y Combinator) that depicts the life cycle of a startup. The graph roughly tracks excitement over time. It begins with a sharp high, the TechCrunch of Initiation, when you get your first press coverage. Right after, however, comes the Trough of Sorrow, a well of discouragement as you struggle to find product-market fit. In Verbling's case, the Trough lasted for more than a year.

One of the reasons why it struggled to find traction was its chicken-and-egg problem, a problem that plagues nearly every marketplace. Traditionally, there are two sides: buyers and sellers. Both are required for a functional marketplace, but early-stage companies must figure out how to attract both sides (or, more commonly, how to attract one side and convince it to stick around long enough for the other side to show up). If anything, Verbling's product made things even harder by requiring the buyer and the seller to be online simultaneously.

Eventually, the company moved forward and solved its product-market-fit problems. Today, Verbling serves as a platform for language learners to improve their language skills using video chat technology. Native language speakers can offer tutoring or teach their own classes. The company was started in 2011 by Jake Jolis, Gustav Rydstedt, and Mikael Bernstein.

GUO: Has Verbling always looked like it does today?

JOLIS: No. Our very first idea was essentially Chatroulette for languages. The idea was we'd pair you via random video chat with a stranger who had the inverse language-learning preferences as you. If you're an American learning Spanish, you'd be matched with a Spaniard learning English. And there would be a timer that would count down from five minutes. Five minutes in one language and then five minutes in the other. Everyone wins, right?

We were getting awful sleep because I would be jolted awake at like four a.m., and there would be a guy in Syria or Iraq trying to practice English. . . . I'd have to turn all the lights on and pretend I was an actual user rather than the cofounder of the company.

We pretty quickly realized that we were building a product with a really difficult chicken-and-egg problem. You need people in different time zones to be matched in real time, who don't speak each other's languages, and who need to have inverse language preferences. So if you, for example, have ten Spanish speakers on one side and one English speaker on the other side, the model breaks, because nine Spanish speakers have to wait to be matched up. It only works if you have massive liquidity on both sides and everyone is matching up across time zones in real time. These days we have a much better, scalable product, but that was where we started.

At first, we only had a few users, so we fought really hard to please the ones that we had. But starting from day one, we had an imbalance of people trying to practice English. It would almost always be the case that we would have people from Latin America, people from the Middle East, people from southern Europe, all trying to practice English. And we didn't have *nearly* enough English users to meet the demand. As it turned out, people wanted to learn English more than English speakers wanted to learn other languages.

GUO: How did you end up solving that problem?

JOLIS: The way that we "solved" it in the early days was to always be online ourselves. We would spend the majority of our days with our little headsets plugged in, being alert in the event that someone would log on. That way, users could at least get paired with us, the founders. It got to the point where I would sleep with my earbuds in so I would hear the site ringing when someone logged on, and I would personally be there and play the part of an English speaker for them. Hopefully users would match with someone else, but if not, I could be there as a backup.

We were in a cheap Sunnyvale apartment, there were Cup Noodles all over the place, and we were getting awful sleep because I would be jolted awake at like four a.m., and there would be a guy in Syria or Iraq trying to practice English. It would often be a bad connection, in the middle of the night. I'd have to turn all the lights on and pretend I was an actual user rather than the cofounder of the company.

That went on for a really long time, and we now refer to it as "the Dark Ages." We couldn't realistically be on 24-7, because we had a lot of other work to do, so it was a common experience for people to sit in what we called "the queue." The queue was complete pandemonium. It was hell. There was a loading icon on the screen, informing you that you were waiting, and it could go on for hours and hours. We would get emails from people saying that they spent hours waiting in the queue and were never matched, and we would feel horrible.

We were really scared of charging [users], I don't know why, but we thought, "We can't charge, it's been free forever, they're going to kill us if we ask for money."

So we eventually pivoted into a marketplace where people could learn languages with real teachers. It's still all video chat, and it's still very much about speaking practice, but now one side pays the other. And now it's awesome. There are classes 24-7; there is always someone there when you want them, day or night, on demand, and users actually love the product.

GUO: How did you get your first hundred or so users?

JOLIS: At first, when we didn't have any users at all, we would try to get bloggers to write about us. We did this in the most obvious way possible: by commenting in bloggers' comments section. This rarely worked. Bloggers just didn't care. However, we knew about one blogger in Madrid, an English teacher, whose blog consistently had hundreds of thousands of readers. We knew that her blog was the best because it was so ultratargeted to the audience that we wanted, but she wouldn't respond to our comments on her blog.

So I finally just went to the store and bought a pen and a paper and an envelope and a stamp. And I wrote this letter to Monica—amazingly, I still remember her name—I wrote the nicest things, but I also said, "Yo, we already dropped out of school to pursue this idea, and we're going to be completely screwed if we don't make this company awesome, and you need to help us or else it's kind of on you." We sent the letter to Spain, to Madrid, and lo and behold she wrote about Verbling. Her blog post gave us an influx of tens of thousands of users.

Another time, my little brother visited and wanted to help, so we gave him the role of finding as many leads as possible. He made accounts on every single language-learning website and started sending messages to anyone he could in order to get them to come to Verbling and talk more. He even made accounts on competitors' websites, trying to convince their users that Verbling was a much better place to practice. Eventually the accounts got shut down, but by that time we had a ton of leads for new users that we could contact.

GUO: What were some things that you tried that didn't work?

JOLIS: Yeah, there were tons of things. One in particular: our very first beta test. I remember I asked my Nicaraguan friend, Nelson, if he could round up all of his Nicaraguan friends to be on the Spanish-speaking side. I had met most of them while traveling to Nicaragua over New Year's once. We then rallied up all of our American college friends to be on the English-speaking side. Then we tried to manually force these two groups to use the platform: we had Americans who didn't really care that deeply about learning Spanish talk to these Nicaraguans who already spoke

English fluently. To their credit, they pretended like they were in fact learning the language to make the test authentic.

The Nicaraguans made a party out of it. They all hung out in the same one house and drank beers and had fun with the whole thing. This would've been great, but when they crammed twenty laptops into the same living room, all hogging the same Wi-Fi, bandwidth became a limiting factor. The connections were bad, and the video quality and latency were horrible. And our friends on both sides had really high standards because they were used to Skype. Many testers could hear mostly crackly voices and people drinking beer. I'm still really thankful for all our patient friends who helped us try the product in the early days.

Every time we got a user who spoke English, we did everything to make them stay. And I still remember the names of these people. We had one user, her name was Judith; she was this lady in Trinidad who was always trying to learn Spanish.

GUO: Describe your experience of building a marketplace.

JOLIS: Marketplaces are very notorious for the chicken-and-egg-problem, but that changes if you already have the chicken. By the time we introduced the paid model, we already had a user base of people we could market to. We were actually really fortunate in that we didn't start from nothing.

In our case, because we had all the students already, we had the demand side covered with all of these students who were already using our free product. So when we hired our first teacher, there was already a huge user base of people that the teacher could target.

We had also raised money at that point, so we could invest in at first paying teachers without charging students to get the whole thing up and running. We could promise the teachers a flat rate and then just have students start using it for free. We were really scared of charging, I don't know why, but we thought, "We can't charge, it's been free forever, they're going to kill us if we ask for money." So we slowly, gradually introduced the monetization.

GUO: What things did you do to recruit teachers?

JOLIS: When we pivoted, we already had hundreds of thousands of users, and if you are a language-learning product, odds are pretty high that a lot of your random learners will happen to also be teachers. So we were able to recruit from our own user base. We would send out mass emails to our own user base asking, "Out of all of you, who is a teacher? Email us and apply to teach and you can make money." That was very effective; a ton of them happened to be teachers. Today, most of our teacher recruitment is inbound.

GUO: With your early users, did you go above and beyond to delight them?

JOLIS: Yeah. Remember, during our very earliest days, our situation was that we were always short on English speakers. Every time we got a user who spoke English, we did everything to make them stay. And I still remember the names of these people. We had one user, her name was Judith; she was this lady in Trinidad who was always trying to learn Spanish. We were so thankful for this person; we would write her nice emails, call her on Skype, and explain how much her using our product actually mattered.

We sent her packages of Verbling T-shirts and all this stuff and made sure that everything she did on Verbling was just awesome. At one point we sent a package to her relative who lived in Miami.

To be frank, it's pretty powerful to now be on the receiving end of some of that. For example, we got a handwritten card from a pediatrician, in Egypt of all places, writing about how much Verbling had helped her. During the Cairo protests, Verbling seemed to have been her escape. Her name is Myriam; you never forget the names of users like that. If you talk to a lot of founders, they can probably tell you the names of users that have affected them in some way.

A lot of people don't know language learning is a big market, because for Americans it's not really a big deal if you know another language, but for the rest of the world, if you know English, it can be the ticket to a better life.

GUO: How has it been transitioning to more scalable processes?

JOLIS: Marc Andreessen has written before about selecting the right market, because if you have a really large market that is really broken, where people are dying for a solution, people will have a lot of patience with your product. They need something so bad they won't really care if it's a little buggy and things aren't perfect, because they so desperately need a solution, and if the market is big enough, a lot of people will still sign up for your service. That was the case for us: in the early days we had a product that wasn't perfect, but the promise of it was great—the promise of instantly connecting with a native speaker so you can practice a new language.

A lot of people don't know language learning is a big market, because for Americans it's not really a big deal if you know another language, but for the rest of the world, if you know English, it can be the ticket to a better life. We got thousands and thousands of sign-ups—even with our early product—and they kind of trickled in throughout our first year because the promise of the product was so good. Then at the end of 2012, when we added on the teachers, everything sort of jumped up a notch and the company really started taking off in terms of usage and revenue and everything. We're on an amazing trajectory now.

But to answer your question, we never really had to actively scale any kind of user acquisition, because it happened through word of mouth very organically, sort of based on the promise of the product, I think. We were lucky to have a lot of press because the concept was kinda novel and easy to understand and very consumer-ish, so journalists liked to write about it. I think the biggest source of the craziness and the biggest reason for our success is that we didn't give up in the year and a half that we were stuck in the shit, so we eventually came up with a way to fix things. That's the reason Verbling works today.

CHAPTER 7: DOORDASH

Tony Xu, Cofounder & CEO

DoorDash enables local food delivery for restaurants (through web and mobile apps), with a larger vision of creating delivery logistics services. Founded in 2013 by Tony Xu, Andy Fang, Stanley Tang, and Evan Charles Moore, the company is the latest in a line of food delivery operators. GrubHub (founded 2004) enabled lookup of local delivery and takeout restaurants, Instacart (founded 2009) enabled delivery services for grocery stores, and a new wave of companies (DoorDash, Fluc, SpoonRocket) are enabling hot meals on demand, one serving at a time.

The great irony of these companies (and one of the great ironies of Silicon Valley) is that today's brilliant business model is yesterday's cautionary tale. Webvan, founded in 1996, was a company that offered online grocery delivery; it went bankrupt in 2001 and is considered one of the biggest dot-com flops in history. Why the rise of on-demand food delivery today? There are many potential explanations, with improved technology (smartphones) and increased expectations (Amazon's next-day and same-day delivery) among them.

Regardless of the reasons, these companies are now competing fiercely for market share. Many are borrowing from Uber's playbook and raising vast amounts of venture capital in order to monopolize the market as quickly as possible. Case in point: in less than two years, DoorDash has raised $60 million in funding and expanded to over a dozen cities across the United States.

GUO: How did you meet your DoorDash cofounders?

XU: We actually met in a class on campus. We met at Startup Garage, which is an entrepreneurship class at Stanford. And we wanted to write software to help small-business owners. That was the principal motivation for the project.

We didn't actually work on the idea for DoorDash in that class. We actually worked on a very different idea. We had worked on a few ideas. The one that we spent the most amount of time on was a product to measure the effectiveness of off-line advertising spending for small-business owners. That's how we got started.

Every night from ten p.m. to two a.m., I would go to the Stanford business school library, and I would print out these seriously ugly flyers that I'd made for restaurants. . . . And over the course of the summer, I printed out well over one hundred thousand flyers.

And actually the advertising product did pretty well. It was just a very simple iPad app that we put on the countertops of small-business owners. Retailers, restaurants, banks—it didn't matter. As long as you have a checkout flow where you have to pay physically in store for something, then you could use the app. And it asks you, "How did you hear about us?" and we would list all the off-line advertising channels. And we'd go door-to-door to put one iPad at different doors. That product did pretty well, but while we were selling it, people kept talking to us about delivery, over and over again.

We ignored it the first couple of times. We didn't really care for it. And then we kind of heard it enough times where we said, "Why are all these people talking about delivery?" When we started doing research, we realized it was about more than just delivering meals to consumers. We asked questions like, "Well, how do they get their own ingredients for restaurants?" or "How does this shoe store get their shoes?" and there always seemed to be a problem with delivery. It didn't matter who the customer was. That was what sparked our interest there.

And we said, "Okay, let's see if the consumers want us for restaurants." So we started with that very simple use case and built a landing page in about two hours with PDF menus and a Google Voice phone number that went to our cell phones. And we got our first order that day after creating that landing page. And that was how it all got started.

GUO: Did you target the landing page at other Stanford students?

XU: No! It wasn't targeted at anyone. It was just PaloAltoDelivery.com. And our first customer—Jeremy is his name. I still know him because I did the delivery. I actually have it all on video on my phone. Basically, he typed "Palo Alto delivery" into his browser, and that was the only way he could have found us, because Google hadn't even indexed us yet. We put it up in two hours. He literally ordered fifty minutes after we set it up.

So it had nothing to do with Stanford. We didn't tell anyone about it. We just said, "Okay. It's up. All right. We'll maybe start driving traffic to it on Monday." This was on a Saturday. This guy Jeremy decided to order pad Thai and some spring rolls. Bangkok Cuisine, I can still remember the restaurant.

GUO: After that, how did you get your next fifty customers?

XU: Okay, so then on Monday, we said, "All right. Let's send this out to Andy and Stanley's dorm mates." We sent it to the dorm [mailing list], which is about, I don't know, two hundred people, something like that. And it wasn't a lot of orders in the beginning. It was two or three maybe trickling in a day.

It was an incredibly manual process. I would download Find My Friends. I would add all of my cofounders' information into Find My Friends so I could track them, and it was only for dinner, because we were in class during lunch. And then we would take turns basically being the dispatcher as well as the driver.

So I would track everyone. I would task them, like, where they have to go, where they need to deliver, and what they need to pick up. This was the dispatch. It was a sheet of paper, a pencil, Find My Friends, and text messaging. And my Google Voice phone. It was just like a pizza shop. You call a number, you get somebody on the other line, and you tell them what you want to order. That's how it worked. I built a very simple Google Form to track all the orders, as well as, "Oh, let me make it so that it's easy to add up the total." So if someone asks, "How much is the bill?" I can tell them how much the bill is.

So that's how it was. That's how sophisticated the menu was and how sophisticated dispatch was. And we did this from February to June of our final year at Stanford, and our highest order count was twenty-one orders on Super Bowl Sunday. I still remember that. It was twenty-one orders over a three-hour window. We didn't do anything but dinner, and that was really hard because it was just the four of us all driving. So we were driving and dispatching basically at the same time. So not a safe exercise, because we were texting and driving and taking phone calls and writing down people's orders. So it wasn't super safe or anything, but that's how we got started.

Getting users after that . . . we hit a snag after a few months, mainly because most of our early customers were Stanford students. They went on vacation, or they decided to intern somewhere, so we lost all of our customers. So during that summer, instead of PaloAltoDelivery.com, we launched DoorDash.com on June 21, 2013.

I found out that a lot of [our early customers] were moms because seventy-seven of them wrote back and told me so. I would literally knock on their doors and ask them why they would use us and where do other moms hang out. And we would go to these events.

That's when we launched at Y Combinator. We had zero customers. And the user acquisition was very door-to-door. We did two things that were of particular interest. One was using my Stanford ID. When you graduate from Stanford, your Stanford ID card is still intact for about four weeks at least. And I took full advantage of that. After graduation, starting the very next day, we would do delivery during the daytime, Andy and Stanley would code during the evening, and then for me, in the wee hours every night from ten p.m. to two a.m., I would go to the Stanford business school library, and I would print out these seriously ugly flyers that I'd made for restaurants. They said, "This restaurant now delivers." I would hand-cut them with the cutters at the Stanford business school library. I'd do this every night for four hours. And over the course of the summer, I printed out well over one hundred thousand flyers.

They were color copies too: 110,000 color copies. To do that at FedEx, even at a discounted rate, it's $33,000. Even with Y Combinator's $20,000, we would have been bankrupt. So to save that money, I did it myself, and I would save every cardboard box that we used in the beginning for larger orders and use them to hold the flyers. I would put them in my trunk, and in the morning I would go door-to-door to each restaurant and distribute them. Because we partner with our restaurants, I would say, "I would really appreciate it if you guys would put this in your takeout bag."

So that was one thing that was very manual to get users that worked well. The second thing was literally going door-to-door. I wrote custom, personalized emails for roughly one thousand customers, and I found out that a lot of them were moms because seventy-seven of them wrote back and told me so. I would literally knock on their doors and ask them why they would use us and where do other moms hang out. And we would go to these events where the moms hung out. We went to a birthing event called Blossom Birth in August. This was also during Y Combinator. We did a lot of these types of things. They were very nonscalable. But that's what we did. There's no easy way to do it in the beginning, to my knowledge.

GUO: At what point did you start transitioning some of these processes to more scalable ones?

XU: It started in Y Combinator because we didn't have a real dispatch system. We kept using the method I told you about, with pencil, paper, Google Docs, Find My Friends, and text messaging, for up to around twenty drivers. We thought maybe our brains could do it for up to five or six drivers, but we did it all the way until twenty drivers out on the road. And then our brains started hurting. We couldn't do it anymore, because it's hard to keep track of twenty people out at once, and then you've gotta track twenty different numbers, and then you've gotta know what place they are in the order process. That ends up being kind of hard, so during this time, we basically automated each step of that flow.

Technology, for all of the fanciness that's perceived in Silicon Valley, at the end of the day, is about solving problems. So we want everyone in this company to understand this particular way of solving a problem.

Step one is like, how do we get the menu from PDF to an actual menu for people to click on? Step two: How do we actually send these orders to these merchants? And some of them, we actually started with an iPad app in which they would receive these orders. That was probably harder than necessary, but we did that. Step three: How do you tell your drivers which order they're on? Step four: How do you get information from the drivers on what their status is? Are they on their way to the restaurant? Are they at the restaurant? Have they picked up from the restaurant? Have they delivered to the customer? Basically we took the entire order process and discretized the steps, and then we tried to automate each component. And then we chose which components to automate first based on how much mental power it took first. That was basically how we did it.

It started that summer and it still continues today on a more sophisticated scale. There were some problems, definitely. The worst thing was that the site would probably crash every day. The site would go down every day for, I don't know, at least thirty minutes to one hour. I remember, almost every day, waking Stanley up at one a.m. because the site went down again. Because you have to remember we're delivering during the day. Between eleven and two, and between five and eight, we're all delivering. And we're writing code from nine p.m. to two a.m., and our brains aren't always fully functional, so we'd make some mistakes. The site went down probably every day during Y Combinator. Well . . . maybe not every day, but at least every other day.

GUO: How did adding users and drivers compare with adding restaurants?

XU: Well, we've always had to recruit restaurants. And in the early days, when I wasn't delivering or printing flyers or stuff like this, I would be selling restaurants. I would go door-to-door on restaurants. I did that in Palo Alto and Mountain View. I sold the first 50 restaurants, and now we have over 1,400 or 1,500; but our first 50, it was just me going door-to-door-to-door, and that's how we did it.

To be honest with you, we learned a lot about our business doing that. Because of that sales process, now I can teach every new salesperson in every new city that we enter. Because every new city is like launching DoorDash all over again, and you have to recruit that first group of restaurants all over again. No one knows about us. Just because we did well in the Bay Area doesn't mean anything for us in LA, and just because we did well in LA doesn't mean anything in Boston.

We just launched in Boston, actually, but we're starting all over again. And we take all the principles we learned early on and we document them, and we change them slightly as we get smarter. Then we replicate them in the new market. As the driver and the sales guy, I actually learned one of the most valuable lessons about selling to small-business owners: because they saw my face all the time, they actually trusted me when I said I could bring them business, because I was *already* bringing them business as the driver.

And I wasn't lying. I really wasn't lying, because they saw my face every time. And that idea of having our drivers be a part of our sales process has made us three to four times more efficient in our selling than any other company out there. We don't need nearly as many salespeople as other companies, because we've got two thousand drivers out on the road, and we can use them for intelligence about how we're doing.

It was very important that we, the founders, were the first to do each job. . . . Because it's very hard to hire somebody and bring them on and motivate, coach, and evaluate them if you don't really understand the job yourself.

GUO: What have you learned from doing all these things manually at the beginning?

XU: Number one, I believe it teaches you that the right way to build a product is not to add feature after feature. The right way to build a product, or what we think is the right way, involves all these processes at work. And the only way to really understand them is to do them manually, and then you decide which ones to automate, and there's various ways you can do that. But that's one thing we really want our people to understand, which is, how do you actually solve a problem? Technology, for all of the fanciness that's perceived in Silicon Valley, at the end of the day, is about solving problems. So we want everyone in this company to understand this particular way of solving a problem.

And the second thing is a sense of humility and empathy for the audience we serve. How hard it can be for the drivers on the road. How hard it is for our merchants or restaurants in terms of making a lot of food with very hungry customers during peak times. How it can be tough as a mom to receive food late if things are busy, because she's got crying children in front of her to worry about. And until you actually do those things, like take those phone calls or deliver those meals, it's hard to really say you understand what each one of those audiences goes through. Those are the two things we're trying to accomplish by having our employees do the manual work.

I think we both know this: in the beginning it's never really glorious. It's maybe a little glorious in Boston, where our launch team is basically the same team that we had in Palo Alto when we got started, and they're just doing it all over again. And one important thing here that we learned is that it was very important that we, the founders, were the first to do each job, whether that meant driving, whether that meant training drivers, whether that meant selling restaurants, whether that meant coding, whether that meant recruiting customers, whatever. Because it's very hard to hire somebody and bring them on and motivate, coach, *and* evaluate them if you don't really understand the job yourself.

Even to this day, we still have that philosophy. I was the first person to launch Los Angeles. I'm going to go and help launch Boston and Chicago. In Boston, we're already off the ground, but I'm still going to go there. And I think that's a very important thing. Not just for morale, but [for] knowing which people to bring onto your team as you get bigger and also how to do the job in general. Because as founders, we're very limited in our experiences or abilities at the onset. We're just young people that don't have that much experience, and the way that you get a little bit smarter is to go and do the job. Do the manual work, and you'll get the experience. And that's how you become, to use Paul Graham's words, formidable. It comes down to just doing the work.

CHAPTER 8: INDINERO

Jessica Mah, Cofounder & CEO

For a lot of entrepreneurs, their first idea isn't always their best. As Teleborder, General Assembly, and Verbling demonstrate, many companies end up working on a different product than the one they first began with. In the case of Jessica Mah and Andy Su, they began with a solution that was primarily product based, but they quickly realized they needed to pivot to services until the product could catch up.

The two founded inDinero from their dorm room in 2009, and they wanted to focus on a problem that they knew was a headache for every single business: accounting. Mah took on unscalable challenges that many founders would shrink from: she studied for and received an IRS Enrolled Agent license in order to manually prepare tax returns herself.

In the years between 2009 and now, a number of other prominent startups have risen to handle similar problems in other domains: ZenPayroll (payroll services) in 2011 and Zenefits (human resources services) in 2012 are just two examples. But inDinero has fought to stay relevant, and today the company provides an all-in-one solution for taxes, payroll, and accounting.

GUO: What did inDinero look like when you first started?

MAH: When we first got started with our primarily software product, we thought, "Let's just set up an office that does all accounting automatically for businesses." The problem was, there was no real way for that to be 100 percent automated. There was always a 10 percent gap in whatever we did, so people would hire bookkeepers to fill in the gap, and eventually the bookkeeper would just undercut us completely and migrate the customer away.

I originally thought, "If I'm ever going to build a $100-million-revenue business, I'll eventually need to hire people to do the accounting work.

That's when we realized, "Holy shit, we have to do something differently." That was around three years ago, and what we said was "Why don't we do all the accounting? Why don't we file the taxes, and we can be an end-to-end solution for our customers?"

So I went out and got my IRS Enrolled Agent license, which allowed me to prepare tax returns and represent taxpayers for tax court. I had to study for a few months in order to get the license. Then we signed up about twenty customers and offered to do all of their accounting and taxes for a few thousand dollars per year. We were basically running an accounting firm with our own software, and we were also preparing our own tax returns. I was the only licensed person to do that in the company.

Eventually, we hired our own full-time accountant, and over time, the software got a lot better. A lot of it now works in an automated way. I don't think we've reached 100 percent, but I don't think we ever will.

GUO: How did you get your first hundred users?

MAH: The first thirty customers I signed up personally. I just found friends that needed accounting help; then I went around and got them all on board one by one. During that process, I wrote down a list of the top hundred questions that I was asked and what my answers were. After about thirty customers, I realized I was hearing the same questions over and over again, which meant that I had compiled an FAQ.

I think at first I was looking for a way to sign up customers through a website, but then we got comfortable with saying, "No, we're going to have a manual sales team." We still do that to this day.

GUO: What was it like studying for your Enrolled Agent license?

MAH: That was pretty interesting. I originally thought, "If I'm ever going to build a $100-million-revenue business, I'll eventually need to hire people to do the accounting work. There's no way to automate it off the bat, though over time we might be able to get our software up to speed. However, in order to hire those people, I need to know how to interview them."

I'm a computer science major, so I knew how to vet an engineering hire to figure out whether or not they knew algorithms and databases. But if I'd not ramped up my accounting and tax knowledge, how would I have been able to really interview accountants; what the hell would I ask? What terminology would I use? If I didn't know myself, I wouldn't be able to hire someone to do that. So I thought, "If I'm going to be studying this, I might as well get licensed."

Simultaneously, we were figuring out that you need someone to sign off on tax returns, and we didn't have the money to hire anyone. And at the time we were starving for cash, down to our last $150–$200K in the bank; we were really fucked. Which made me decide to pull the trigger. During the day I would talk to customers and sell them on inDinero, and at night I would read through a textbook I bought. I was spending two to three hours a day cramming for tests. It wasn't just one test, either. There are three you have to pass to get licensed. Honestly it was a big pain in the ass, but it was worth it.

During the day I would talk to customers and sell them on inDinero, and at night I would read through [an IRS Enrolled Agent] textbook I bought. I was spending two to three hours a day cramming for tests.

GUO: What prompted you to consider the pivot to tax services?

MAH: Customer engagement and long-term retention were awfully low. Most customers were gone after a three-month period. We weren't really solving the problem for them, because we said we would automate everything away, but they still had to do a lot of work. What we were promising didn't match what we were providing.

On top of that, even if we had delivered on the bookkeeping side, we weren't handling end-to-end work on the tax side. So I called up a lot of customers saying, "Hey, I know you work near us. Can I drive to your office and watch you use inDinero? I really want to see what you think: the good, bad, and ugly." I went to so many offices and met so many interesting, kind, supportive people. That's really what led us to figuring out how to change course.

GUO: Were any of those one-on-ones memorable?

MAH: Yeah, I remember one guy whose company was just raking in the cash; they were doing more than $1 million in annual revenue at the time. So I thought, "Wow, they've got a pretty good business now; why are they using inDinero?" And he told me, "Jess, I really like inDinero, but I make a lot of money and frankly inDinero is not doing everything perfectly. I would pay a shitload more money if I could just press a button and say, 'File my taxes for me.' I'd pay a few thousand dollars to do that, and I'd love it if that was an option." That's when I had the lightbulb, saying, "We should totally offer that." That was one of the customer interactions that I could really consider "customer development." It even inspired me to talk to more customers.

We tried billions of things [for user acquisition]. I tried paying for ads, but people don't find accountants via Google AdWords.... Which isn't to say that it never works—it's just something we tried that didn't work.

GUO: Were there any things you tried for user acquisition that didn't work?

MAH: We tried billions of things. I tried paying for ads, but people don't find accountants via Google AdWords. They find accountants through a trusted referral. Which isn't to say that it never works—it's just something *we* tried that didn't work.

I tried to have accountants sell inDinero services. I thought, "Oh, why don't I get accountants who want extra money, and since they know accounting, they can sell accounting!" That ended up being total bullshit. Accountants are horrible salespeople; they don't know what to do to close customers. We tried again, but instead of teaching an accountant sales, we taught an experienced salesperson taxes and accounting. And that ended up working.

GUO: Did you do anything to go above and beyond for your earliest users?

MAH: Well, a lot of them were personal friends of mine, so I visited most of them in person at that point. Over time, I don't think I've done as good of a job with that, if I'm being honest. I never went so far as to write handwritten holiday cards; it just didn't happen. You've gotta pick and choose your battles.

Early on we only offered accounting and tax services, and I had one customer on the phone say, "Hey, if you guys offered payroll, I'd pay you twice as much money." At this point my cofounder and I were literally surviving on Cup Noodles, so I said, "Great question; let me put you on hold for a second!" I put him on hold and I asked my cofounder, "Hey, do we offer payroll? A customer's offering us $200 more a month." Which was how inDinero started doing taxes *and* payroll, all under one roof.

GUO: How has it been transitioning to more automated systems?

MAH: It's really not as easy and straightforward as I thought. I thought we'd figure it out after a couple of years, and we're making some great progress. Which is totally fine considering the timeline. There's a lot of ground to cover. There are no big players here other than QuickBooks. But it's really difficult.

Even a year and a half ago, we said, "What are we going to do about this? We can't just keep hiring accountants in excess; we're going to bankrupt ourselves. Most of these people, they don't even want to be doing this kind of work." That's how our Manila office got started. We hired some contractors online; they were from the Philippines and they were getting really good work done. We did some research, and we found out that a ton of people in the Philippines want to be accountants. It was perfect.

As we accumulated more accountants over there, we figured we'd start hiring engineers out there too. We'd been trying to hire engineers in SF, and it just wasn't going well. It was difficult to attract really smart people, because they'd say, "Accounting software? That sounds a little boring." But in the Philippines, we've been able to hire computer science grads that are really passionate about building inDinero. Since all of our accountants are out there, we can have them working side by side with the engineers to iron out the software kinks. That's really key. If they were in the Bay Area, if would be harder to do that, actually.

Today we've grown to 120 employees in San Francisco, the Philippines, and in Portland, Oregon. For better or for worse, we think of ourselves sort of like a factory. We still have a lot of factory workers, but they help us figure out how to build the robots that build everything in the car for us. But the best car companies can't outsource their workers. Their factory workers are not just "factory workers"—they're like real technicians. That was something we took inspiration from and decided to institute ourselves. So all of our workers are full-time inDinero employees.

CHAPTER 9: ZENEFITS

Parker Conrad, Cofounder & CEO

Zenefits is a modern HR company that's aiming to be the one place to connect and manage all of your HR services. The company was founded in 2013 by Parker Conrad and Laks Srini, years after similar companies such as ZenPayroll (payroll services), inDinero (accounting and tax services), and Workday (HR services).

Despite being around for only two years, Zenefits is currently valued at a staggering $4.5 billion (as of May 2015). As you might expect, the company has had an unbelievable growth trajectory so far, and it has been labeled the "fastest-growing SaaS company ever."[1] One of the most fascinating lessons that Zenefits has learned is that growth trumps nearly everything. While this is certainly true from a fundraising perspective, for Zenefits it has proven to be true from a business perspective as well; they have solved some truly intractable problems simply by growing at a mind-boggling rate.

---

1. "Labeled the 'fastest growing SaaS company ever,' Zenefits raises a $66M Series B just five months post-Series A," Michael Carney, June 2014, https://pando.com/2014/06/03/labeled-the-fastest-growing-saas-company-ever-zenefits-raises-a-66m-series-b-just-five-months-post-series-a/.

To help put that growth rate in perspective: Zenefits and DoorDash are the second- and third-youngest companies in this book, but their valuation put together ($5.1 billion, as of 2015) dwarfs that of every other startup here *combined*. It's a striking (but not uncommon) example of Silicon Valley's power-law distribution: the big winners are so big that they overshadow the returns from most other companies, including small and medium winners.

GUO: What did Zenefits look like when it first launched?

CONRAD: When we first launched, our product let companies enroll in health insurance online. You could see quotes and prices, pick a plan, and enroll in it without leaving the site. It also integrated with your payroll system to generate individual pricing and set up employee deductions.

At the time, we were actually racing another company in our Y Combinator batch. It was called SimplyInsured. Originally it was fairly different from us, but about halfway through YC, the founders decided that they wanted to do what we were doing, and the company pivoted into our market.

So we found ourselves sprinting to be the first ones out the door. Because the first company that launched would be summarized as "Company XYZ launches to make insurance benefits simpler for small businesses," and whoever launched a couple weeks later would get "Company ABC seems to be derivative of XYZ and does the same thing and why are they doing the same thing as Company XYZ?" It wouldn't matter that we had started our product first if they launched theirs first.

The feature set of that first product had two sections. The first let employers pick plans and fill out necessary application forms. The second let employees choose a plan from the ones

> *The most intractable area of [HR]—the hardest systems to deal with—are the insurance ones. They're all stuck in 1986. And for companies with fewer than a hundred employees, they don't accept anything other than faxes to make changes to add or remove employees.*

their employer offered. Both of these parts are critical, as you need both in order to fully enroll a company in insurance. But because we were panicked about SimplyInsured, we wanted to just launch *something* in order to get out the door. So when we had our launch article in TechCrunch, the only thing we had built was the employer portion of the product.

Literally half the product didn't exist yet. But we figured that nobody was going to dive so deep into the product that they would actually get to the employee stage. You had to fill out an entire form and pick a plan and get all the way through the employer application before you got to the point where you emailed your employees. So we reasoned that most companies would stop on the page for picking different plans and want to talk to us. That gave us at least a couple of days after we launched to get the second part built.

In case we were wrong, if they got all the way through, we had a blank page that said, "Thanks, we'll be in touch with the next steps." So we launched with that, and then for two weeks our second half of the product literally didn't exist. But it got us out the door first. And if you go back and look at our news coverage, it was something like "Zenefits is doing this really interesting thing for small businesses around health insurance." And then a

> *Most brokers barely know how to use email. For them, handing a client a bunch of forms and having the client fax them in to the insurance company is the easiest thing in the world.*

couple weeks later SimplyInsured launched, and the article about them was "Second company doing same thing as Zenefits and unclear if it's different or better." It ended up being great press for us but terrible press for them.

GUO: What were some of the scaling challenges you faced early on?

CONRAD: One thing that I've learned is that with a lot of things which at first seem totally unscalable, once you spend enough time thinking about them, you figure out ways to get to scale. We still have to go back and build out automated systems, and that takes time, but there were a bunch of problems for us that went from totally unsolvable to pretty feasible after enough time and with enough resources.

One great example of that is how we work with insurance companies themselves. The way I think about our product is as a hub-and-spoke system for HR software; today, you have twenty different systems related to your employees and none of them are connected, which creates this massive administrative problem for companies. When you hire or terminate someone, you need to add or remove them from twenty different systems, and when something changes in their life, you need to make adjustments to all of these different systems individually, often manually, via a fax machine.

The most intractable area of that—the hardest systems to deal with—are the insurance ones. They're all stuck in 1986. And for companies with fewer than a hundred employees, they don't accept anything other than faxes to make changes to add or remove employees. It's all on paper, all via fax machine. And it's actually even worse than that, because not only are they using fax machines, but they're unreliable in processing information. When you send them a fax to make a change, 90 percent of the time they do their job correctly, but 10 percent of the time the fax will come out the other end and whoever is in charge of processing that day had too much work to do and it got lost in the shuffle and it never happened, or they typed it in wrong and someone added employee A to company B and added employee B to company A, and you actually need to call and follow up and close the loop with every change that you make with the insurance company.

You have to pick up the phone and make sure it was done correctly, and that's the ultimate thing that doesn't scale. When we raised our Series A, that was one of the big questions: Is there any way to make this insurance stuff scale? We knew it was going to be a complete nightmare. And honestly, we weren't sure how to do it.

But one of the really cool things that happened for us was that even though we launched at the end of April in 2013, by January 2014 we had actually become the largest insurance broker in the state of California for new businesses. It was with Anthem Blue Cross, which is the largest carrier in the state.

This is interesting because insurance companies are not used to seeing their brokers grow that quickly. They looked at their top twenty or so brokers, and most of those guys have been in that top-twenty list for thirty years or longer. And we went from nonexistent to number one after eight months. They couldn't believe it, and suddenly we had a lot of VP-level people from all these different insurance carriers coming by our office and trying to understand how it happened. They asked us, "Hey, how can we work more closely with you guys; what can we do to get more business from you?"

The thing we always like to tell them is we want electronic integration with their systems to make changes with plans, to add new employees, to make changes to company information—all of the stuff to make it happen electronically without paperwork on our end.

What happens right now if you're a customer of ours is you go through a nice online flow of benefits, and then our system has to generate a paper form, which we then fax in. You never see this—this goes on behind the scenes—but we fax it in and then someone picks up the phone and makes sure everything happens, and follows up to correct any mistakes.

But we're about to launch integrations with all of the major insurance carriers in California to do all of that stuff electronically, and they've never done this before for smaller companies, because none of their brokers wanted to do it that way. Most brokers barely know how to use email. For them, handing a client a bunch of forms and having *the client* fax them in to the insurance company is the easiest thing in the world. So that's how insurance companies were operating until now.

We're single-handedly moving that market online. And the carriers have built a lot of these electronic systems for us specifically. Without that, we would have never figured out how to make the insurance process scale, never in a million years. But lo and behold, if you grow quickly enough, suddenly even your intractable problems are solvable. Suddenly people wanted to work with us, and solutions started to present themselves.

> *[For] the things we thought would not scale, we ended up finding creative ways to make them scale. And a lot of things, a lot of areas we didn't think would be problematic, we found massive bottlenecks that we didn't expect.*

GUO: Did you have other manual systems behind the scenes early on?

CONRAD: Definitely. In general we do a lot of stuff that doesn't scale, and in fact one of the things that I found with our company growing is everything that I do all day is largely about trying to make things that don't really scale, scale.

It's true for different parts of our system. In fact, none of our forms were automated at first. What would happen is someone would go through the online system and enroll in insurance and we'd get an email saying, "So-and-so completed . . . ," and we would pull a database extract of all their answers and fill out the form by hand. We originally hired someone to sort of deal with that, but over time it became mechanized. The PDF became automatically generated with all of the information filled out and signature attached to the bottom.

And over time this became more and more meta. What we would do is, at first, we would manually fill the forms. Then we would automate form filling, but we would manually set up the automation. But every insurance carrier in every state has separate forms for all these different transactions. So they have their own forms, and you need to automate each of them separately in the system. It got to the point where we were spending all of our time automating forms. So we wrote software to automate form automation, so someone nontechnical could go in and upload a form and just point out which part of the form to fill out with which information.

So we went from manually doing each individual form to automating forms to automating the process of automating forms, and now we're moving towards the system where there are no forms at all.

GUO: Has there been anything surprising about the way you've had to automate these processes?

CONRAD: With a lot of the things that *seem* scalable, you will find bottlenecks you never imagined that you suddenly need to find solutions for. For example, the way we were generating our list of companies to reach out to—there was a manual step in this process where someone had to copy and paste information into an Excel spreadsheet. We got to a point where that person could not physically do their copy-paste job fast enough, and the growth of the company was literally constrained by this person's ability to load the information into Excel and then our marketing software. Never in a million years did we think that would be a bottleneck for us. So we had to automate a lot of the process and build software around that.

Something similar happened with the way we set up clients in our system. We need to load a lot of data initially for new companies, like what insurance plans the company offers, the benefit levels, the deductible, copay, cost, etc. And the pricing data can be fairly complex because it's not simply a flat rate of X dollars.

It might be different based on the employee's age or zip code, so you need to have prices for each plan for every possible zip code and age.

So it's essentially a lot of data that we're loading. We enter in other information too, all these other things like "What's the waiting period?" or "How much can the company contribute?" And when new employees use the system, we can tell them how much it costs, what percentage they pay versus their employer, when they become eligible, all of that stuff.

The process for setting those plans up in the system was fairly manual. First it was just done by the engineering team, back when we were getting two to three clients a week, and that was feasible. And then the volume of clients started growing. We had a team of people that would prepare the information for the engineering team, formatted properly, so the engineering team could run one script and load it in. And that became a miserable disaster as we scaled—there were so many errors, the data was never quite right, and the engineering team was like, "Why the fuck are they sending us data that isn't clean?"

At one point, we could set up plans for six to eight new customers per day, but we were adding about eighteen new customers into the back of the pipe every day, so there was this very rapidly increasing bottleneck. By the end of June of that year we had to tell potential customers that we could not get them up and running with insurance until September or October. And obviously that's unacceptable if you're a company; if you want insurance you generally want it *now*.

There was this massive backlog. Even worse, there were companies that we hadn't told about this delay because we didn't know about it until it hit us—it was an "oh shit" moment—so we threw our entire engineering team at this issue. In about two weeks we built this plan system tool, and on the first day the team that used it loaded sixty-five plans. Totally unclogged all the pipes. It eliminated plan loading as a bottleneck, but of course the bottleneck moved somewhere else.

Even though we launched at the end of April in 2013, by January 2014 we had actually become the largest insurance broker in the state of California for new businesses. . . . Insurance companies are not used to seeing their brokers grow that quickly. They looked at their top twenty or so brokers, and most of those guys have been in that top-twenty list for thirty years or longer.

What happened for us is that this year we've really hired up the engineering team and launched very little in terms of new features because everyone has been focused on making things that don't scale, scale. That sucked up a lot of our engineering resources after the fact.

Anyway, all of this was a long way of saying that, [for] the things we thought would not scale, we ended up finding creative ways to make them scale. And a lot of things, a lot of areas we didn't think would be problematic, we found massive bottlenecks that we didn't expect.

GUO: What have you learned from dealing with Zenefits' massive growth?

CONRAD: Ultimately if things are working well—and from a demand perspective, things are working well for us—what happens is that the entire focus of a company becomes about how to make things scale: how to make customer support scale, implementation scale; how to make account management scale; how to make sales and marketing scale. It all comes down to making things scale. That's the only thing I do in my job, really, other than a little bit of product work.

And it's a lot easier to figure out how to scale something that doesn't feel like it would scale than it is to figure out what is actually gonna *work*. You're much better off going after something that will work [but] doesn't scale, then trying to figure how to scale it up, than you are trying to figure it all out. That's why I think PG's advice is pretty dead-on.

That's what it comes down to, ultimately; it's so much easier to be focused on that once you know what works. And until you have something that is *actually* working, it doesn't matter.

CHAPTER 10: ZEROCATER

Arram Sabeti, Founder & CEO

In November of 2009, Arram Sabeti was hatching his idea for ZeroCater within the belly of another startup, Justin.tv. Sabeti started ZeroCater by solving his own problems; he was responsible for Justin.tv's lunch catering, and he converted his daily headache into an opportunity. Today ZeroCater makes it dead simple for businesses to cater meals by sourcing from local pop-up kitchens, gourmet food trucks, restaurants, private chefs, and caterers. Although there are a number of companies currently that deal with interfacing with the real world (see General Assembly, Teespring, FlightCar, and DoorDash), ZeroCater got its start *much* earlier than the rest.

ZeroCater is a business that provides value by taking care of "schlep": a tedious, unpleasant task. Many engineers actively avoid schleps, assuming that they can generate success by writing code and not getting their hands dirty. Sabeti, however, realized early on that in his business, schleps are inevitable. Indeed, the whole point of this book is that for nearly every meaningful business, schleps are inevitable.

GUO: You were at Justin.tv before you started ZeroCater, right?

SABETI: Yeah. So I actually originally joined Justin.tv entirely because I wanted to have an apprenticeship before I started my own company. I ended up applying to a bunch of startups, and Justin.tv was the one that I got all the way through the process with. And I explained at the first interview that I was just there for the experience, and I didn't care how much they paid me. I also told them, "Just to give you fair warning, I'm gonna quit in a year and start my own company." I didn't get hired for that job. But I *was* hired for a different position that they created for me.

I explained at the [Justin.tv] interview that I was just there for the experience, and I didn't care how much they paid me. I also told them, "Just to give you fair warning, I'm gonna quit in a year and start my own company."

I ended up being there for almost two years. At some point I realized that my original yearlong deadline has passed, so I gave myself a new deadline of six months to grow an idea to profitability, so I could work on it full time. I considered a few ideas, and looking back they were probably pretty bad ones. But as it turned out, the biggest pain I had at the time was actually ordering meals inside of Justin.tv. It was this constant firefighting, and people weren't happy and the portions weren't right, and restaurants would forget to deliver and they wouldn't send enough food. It was just a huge, huge pain in the ass.

GUO: What was it about ZeroCater that made it an appealing idea?

SABETI: Well, I could do it manually, which was important because I wasn't an engineer and I wasn't about to write my software. I think you can argue that having constraints is an asset sometimes, and in this case it probably was an asset. If I had had the ability to just write a Twitter clone, there might have been a serious danger of me doing that.

In fact, there was a company recently which originally was "an API for restaurants" before they pivoted away from that. And when I asked them why, they said, "You know, we just couldn't figure out how to get away from having to pick up the phone." But to make something like this work, you have to be willing to pick up the phone; you have to be willing to do the schleppy, annoying stuff.

In general, though, I'd recommend people learn how to write software.

It got to the point where I was spending literally ten or twenty hours a week manually creating invoices. . . . I don't recommend that at all. . . . It just kills your brain; it's terrible.

GUO: After Justin.tv, where did you get your next customer?

SABETI: Actually, Justin Kan is one of the founders of Justin.tv, which became Twitch.tv, and when I told him that I wanted to do this, he introduced me to the CEO of Scribd. And the CEO of Scribd introduced me to Scribd's office manager, and I went and had a conversation with her. I basically told her, "Hey, I want to take over this responsibility from you." She didn't even think about it, she just said, "Oh, that sounds amazing; let's do that." And it was good to have some outside validation that I had found a problem people cared about.

At that point I just started doing it one step at a time. I didn't really have any process; I didn't have any relationships or vendor partners. I just was calling restaurants up one by one, and saying, "Hey, I want to place a catering order with you, and I want to order $500 of food. Can you give us a discount for that?" Because the way our model works is that we negotiate volume discounts with vendors, which become our margin.

We didn't do anything super clever for user acquisition, to be totally honest. We had really good word-of-mouth growth; we have a direct-sales team right now, as well, so that's it. It's direct sales and word of mouth.

GUO: How did you bring on new customers back then?

SABETI: It was just a conversation. The idea behind ZeroCater is that if somebody can pass us a few parameters, the tool will run automatically. So they start off by requesting something simple like, "We have five vegetarians, two vegans, and one person with a peanut allergy out of twenty-two people, and we want lunch at noon every day."

And that just becomes a standing order; we reuse that information. Of course, they can add more to it. They can say, "We like healthy food," or "We like lots of meat," or "We don't like ethnic food." It can be anything, and I've seen some really weird dietary preferences. My favorite is probably "We can eat eggs, but we don't want to *see* eggs."

GUO: How did you manage schedules and deliveries?

SABETI: A fistful of spreadsheets, and manual emailing. To send a single order I developed this process where you had to copy and paste from multiple spreadsheets. I had a schedule spreadsheet that generated text that I would put in the email subject, which would tell all the information about when and where the order needed to be. Then I had another spreadsheet with the details for the saved order and the individual prices and the subtotals and the tax and all that stuff, and I'd type all of it into the body and then I'd send that off, and that would be an order.

It was just an extremely arduous process of copying and pasting from a dozen different places, making sure no errors creeped in and that formulas were all in their proper places.

GUO: What was your experience working with existing restaurant systems?

SABETI: Honestly, the answer to that question is, what systems?

The difficult thing about our business is that we can do this incredible song and dance, and ultimately the vendor on the other side can just not follow through. So we now do three levels of confirmation for every single order. We make them click a link online, we do an automated phone call check-in the day before, and when they deliver it, we expect them to type in a pin to indicate that the food's actually arrived.

The original version of the confirmation had them reply "Finished" to the email I sent them, and I'd put a check mark in this big spreadsheet I had of all the orders I'd sent out. It had all this nice conditional formatting in Excel where if it was an x it was red, if it was a y it was green, and I'd just go down the list and see who hadn't replied yet and follow up with them. I'd call them—"Hey, did you get that order?"—and that was the process. But things kept falling through the cracks, and so I would add another level of confirmation; I'd start calling the day before for orders to make sure that they hadn't forgotten about them, and it just took a while to develop the process.

GUO: How long did you maintain those spreadsheets and manual phone calls?

SABETI: It was a pretty significant amount of time. It got to the point where I was spending literally ten or twenty hours a week manually creating invoices. And that felt terrible. I don't recommend that at all. I brought on the first programmer to start automating things, and after he helped me do the first couple of rounds manually, he said, "Wow, this is harder than programming!" It just kills your brain; it's terrible.

The first thing we automated was the billing system, because that was the most painful thing at the time. I remember the first day that we pressed the button to generate the invoices, and it took like two seconds to finish, and I said, "Oh, my God, this is the best age you could possibly be living in in the history of humanity!" Because I'd been spending ten or twenty hours a week doing this by hand, and then we wrote some software to do it in three seconds.

In the beginning there was definitely a sense of "Can I really do this? Is this allowed, for me to just start the service, to charge people for this thing that I'm doing from all these spreadsheets?"

GUO: Was it easy to transition away from the manual processes?

SABETI: Well, we still have some manual processes to this day. Some of our tasks are very particular, and at least for now computers aren't as good at curating menus as people are. So creating a menu for the first time and saying, "I'm gonna put item X and item Y together, and that's going to make a good coherent meal overall," that's still a lot of human touch involved. Today, other people have taken over planning the daily menus, but I still personally do the calendar planning, which is the scheduling and proper spacing of different orders. We make sure that there isn't any repetition, or that customers don't receive similar types of food too close together.

GUO: Looking back, what's something that surprises you about the early days?

SABETI: It's kind of hard to remember now, because it just seems so silly, but in the beginning there was definitely a sense of "Can I really do this? Is this allowed, for me to just start the service, to charge people for this thing that I'm doing from all these spreadsheets?" And throughout the answer was yes, but it was a mental transition to get to "I can go and charge people."

Mainly because at the beginning it didn't feel like I had a sense of legitimacy. I was literally just one guy with a handful of spreadsheets, making all this stuff up as he went, and negotiating deals on the fly to get this to work with the vendors, and I felt a little weird about it at first.

CHAPTER 11: TEESPRING

Walker Williams, Cofounder & CEO

Traditionally, T-shirt companies have not been a great domain for startups, from both founders' and investors' perspectives. Selling T-shirts has such a low barrier to entry that market differentiation is difficult, and without an expert in supply chain management, inventory costs can quickly destroy a nascent company. With Teespring, Walker Williams and Evan Stites-Clayton managed to flip that model on its head.

Teespring allows anyone to design and sell custom apparel. Taking cues from other crowdfunding sites like Kickstarter, the company can enable customers to achieve economies of scale without taking on the risk of inventory; the shirts are made only if the crowdfunding goal is reached, and Teespring doesn't have to pay for large print runs in advance.

Although the fundamental model has proven successful, ironing out the kinks has been an interesting experience. The company was founded in 2011, and since then Williams and Stites-Clayton have had to deal with logistics nightmares and fulfillment challenges. As a result, however, they have created a massive operation, which printed seven million T-shirts in 2014.

GUO: Where did you come up with the idea for Teespring?

WILLIAMS: I was a senior at Brown at the time, doing freelance design, freelance development—lots of stuff. I also had a company at the time, which I had taken through an incubator with my cofounder, Evan Stites-Clayton, who was also at Brown.

Our senior year of college, the local dive bar on campus got shut down. It was called the Fish Company, and this was *the* institution for students, because every Wednesday night all of the freshmen and sophomores would go to what they called Fish Co.

I think we found that, for most companies, [growth is] a whole lot harder in practice than it is in theory. Nobody really has the meteoric up-and-to-the-right launch where everything seems so simple. It's always a battle early on.

So when it got raided and shut down, there was this massive outpouring of energy and support. People were talking about it on Twitter, on Facebook, on the student blogs, and in the student paper. It was sort of the end of an era. And Evan and I saw that energy, and we wanted to do something around it that was entrepreneurial in the sense that we wanted to make money, but we also wanted to capture the energy that we saw.

In the fast news cycle of today, there are these stories that reach a fever pitch, and then two weeks later they're out of sight and out of mind. It's not that the story becomes less important to people, it's just that there is so much new news, this constant stream, and something else has taken the crowd. So on a whim we said, "You know what would be great? Let's create a 'Remember the bar' shirt."

We designed something simple and threw it on Facebook. We got a bunch of likes, called a local screen printer, and said, "Design people seem to like it. We want to print it out; how do we do that?" And of course the response was "Well I need to know exactly how many you need, exactly what sizes, and at that point you're going to have to pay me up front, and it'll be about $1,000." Then two weeks later you get a big box, and figuring out the rest is up to you.

Obviously, none of that worked for me. I didn't have the money, even if I wanted to do it myself, and two weeks is an eternity. It just wasn't an ideal solution. And we looked at other options, but nothing really got us to the highest quality prints. Just before we gave up, we decided to see if we could get two hundred preorders. If we could, we would print and individually ship the shirts out. But only if we reached that two hundred mark where it was worth it. Where we knew that people actually wanted it.

So we created a really simple website—it's still up today—called FreeFishCo.com. We put it together in a day—six hours of coding. Very, very simple. It was completely bare bones, and we got it out that night. Within twenty-four hours, we had sold hundreds of products, made a good amount of money, and more importantly we had *tons* of outreach from various student groups on campus. The charity groups like Relay for Life, the frats, the art students—just very different cross sections of campus. So we knew there was something there. Especially considering that we hadn't created a platform; we had just made a simple one-page website and people had taken a leap of logic. And never before in anything that we had done had we seen that dynamic develop. So we immediately knew there was something there. We didn't quite know what it was, but that was the point that we decided that we could do something with this.

GUO: What did the next few campaigns after that look like?

WILLIAMS: You know, it was a battle. So we "started" the company after we had the idea, but we really started the company once we graduated. We raised a little bit of money from investors from the previous business who were really excited about us, and we got to work. I think we found that, for most companies, it's a whole lot harder in practice than it is in theory. Nobody really has the meteoric up-and-to-the-right launch where everything seems so simple. It's always a battle early on.

Our first customers were really the results of grinding. First we went to the people in our network: anybody we knew, anybody that had a connection to a nonprofit, or a group that could potentially buy T-shirts, or friends who might be in the area. And we found out early on that because the product needed work, and because we had a lot to figure out on our side, it was definitely not a scalable business.

I always talk about [startups] as pushing a boulder up a hill. At the beginning, it is the hardest when you reach the steepest incline. But after a certain point it becomes easier and easier, until a point at which the boulder starts to roll.

It was something where we were absolutely fixated on giving the customer the best experience. And in doing so for a local nonprofit, we did things like make lots of calls, we did the design work for them, and we managed the campaign for them. They would basically just promote it and get a check. And after all those meetings and all that work, it only sold something like fifty or sixty shirts. Early on we definitely looked like the opposite of a scalable business. But it was worth it because we built up customers that were happy with us, who knew us, who liked what we had to offer, and over time it compounded on itself.

I always talk about it as pushing a boulder up a hill. At the beginning, it is the hardest when you reach the steepest incline. But after a certain point it becomes easier and easier, until a point at which the boulder starts to roll. I think building a startup is essentially a series of hills. And our first hill, we got over it by doing whatever it took to get a customer and make that customer happy.

GUO: What did the end-to-end process look like back then?

WILLIAMS: It was all manual. It was very, very manual. We would put together the designs and images. We had one printer that we were working with. We'd put together the images and essentially we would manually organize it. Someone on our team at the time—there were only four of us—someone at the business would literally call in and order the shirts from the printer. He had to call the printer and let them know what was coming. We'd get on the phone and tell the printer how it should look. It was so manual, and I think it was the right way to do it. Because we didn't have any idea of who we were trying to build for. We didn't know who our customers were at the time.

GUO: Which parts of the business have moved from manual to automated?

WILLIAMS: Well, automating takes a long time. There is always a trade-off, and it's been very painful to correct all this technical debt. And to correct the sort of duct tape features in the business.

In a way, that's a problem of success. I wouldn't necessarily say, "Make sure you build it to scale to millions and millions of users right away," because realistically you don't need to. Your goal should be to think about the next order of magnitude. So it was a painful process; it probably slowed us down and made us work for a period of more than twelve months at essentially half pace. With every step we took, we sort of took a half step back, because we had to fix things that were broken or not scalable.

But in the end it allowed us to catapult so fast, that duct tape code, even though we had this period of correction and slowness. Even though we had this feeling of "If we would have done this right the first time we wouldn't be in this mess," I don't know if we would have been able to support the growth or keep up with the business had we not done it the way we did. It was a necessary evil, that catch-up period.

GUO: Is there an example of when you realized you had outgrown a manual process?

WILLIAMS: Yeah, I mean originally Teespring was designed where somebody could launch *one* product, like a blue T-shirt. Today, you can sell the same design on a blue T-shirt, or a red hoodie, or a green women's tank top. You know, you get a variety of options. When we first figured that out, that people wanted to sell with these variations, we didn't have the code to do it, and the system wasn't set up to make that easily accessible.

So for a period of six months we would manually add product variations. In our admin panel, we built a really shitty way for people to add products into a campaign. And for six months during some of our more intense growth, we had a team of people spending a vast majority of their day adding products. It got to around ten people who would just be adding products to campaigns. Users had to write emails that would say, "Add a green

T-shirt to this and add a purple hoodie to this for this price and this price," and we would just do it by hand.

That's just one example, but there is a lot of stuff like that. Even now, we still have a lot of manual things that we will eventually correct, but again, they're a necessary evil.

I think the biggest aspect to delighting users is just being there when things inevitably go wrong. So we had a policy that no matter how dire a shape the business was in, we would always make it right.

GUO: What else did you do to delight your earliest users?

WILLIAMS: Honestly, I think the biggest aspect to delighting users is just being there when things inevitably go wrong. So we had a policy that no matter how dire a shape the business was in, we would always make it right. And there were times we didn't have a lot of money to spare, where things were tight, and we would get something wrong, where something would be misspelled or the colors would be slightly off and they really cared about the colors or it was slightly too small. Or even things that most people would look at and say, "That's not enough to spend tens of thousands of dollars on fixing." But we always forced ourselves to do it.

And it made me very conscious of our process, and to not accept things that were wrong with it. When you end up having to pay thousands of dollars to correct a mistake, you look at what the root cause of the mistake was, and you really make sure it doesn't happen again. So we always went above and beyond to make sure our customers were happy. It went across the board. If a customer is selling thirty to fifty shirts, giving them free design and a campaign manager and helping them set up their campaign probably isn't worth it, right? But those are your early customers. They are going to deal with the most friction and mistakes, so giving them that extra level of attention is worth it. Even though the logical approach might be to say, "This customer is worth $1,000; I can only spend a few hundred dollars." Our approach was more "What do we need to do to make this customer thrilled with their experience?"

I remember one time I got a request from a client, a really good long-term client, who wanted to sell something other than T-shirts. They wanted to sell bobbleheads, but they didn't know how to ship them or print them. So we organized the production, but when it came time to ship, there was no easy way to do it because we didn't know the necessary shipping requirements. And as those products arrived we quickly realized there wasn't a person we could call who would come in, package them, and ship them out. So after work one day me and a couple of guys got in the car and drove an hour and a half north of Petaluma, and we packed bobbleheads until after midnight. Just to make sure the customer was happy.

GUO: How has your printing and distribution process changed?

WILLIAMS: Right now we have printers that do the fulfillment and distribution, but we are building out our own facility where we will do our own print-and-ship. We'll still work with our partners; it will just be to help with the growth and enable a few other interesting things. So today we have a system to train our printers, to figure out what works so they actually print and ship the products out.

GUO: What was the process for signing up new printers?

WILLIAMS: We would just find a crew we really liked—and I think we got lucky with our first few printers—and we would ask them, "Who are the best people in the industry?" And then we would call those printers, go in and give them a couple of sample jobs to make sure that we loved the quality, and we'd recruit them. We'd also ask other people who were buying a lot of T-shirts to print on. We'd ask those people, "Who are the best printers that you guys know? Who do you go to for samples?" So we just looked for any way to find the highest quality vendors.

Always focus on the next order of magnitude. Don't overthink growth or scalability. Don't be worried about your thousandth user when you don't have your first.

GUO: What's something you've learned about having to manage such incredible growth?

WILLIAMS: Always focus on the next order of magnitude. Don't overthink growth or scalability. Don't be worried about your thousandth user when you don't have your first. And don't be worried about your millionth user before you have your hundred thousandth. You shouldn't try to build for success you don't have. It's much better to be so successful that you can't keep up, you can't keep the website up, rather than being stuck with a product that scales to ten million users when you have ten thousand.

CHAPTER 12: CODECADEMY

Ryan Bubinski, Cofounder & CEO

Less than eight months after General Assembly was founded, and less than a year before online university giants Coursera and Udacity were announced, a new player in the online programming-education space reared its head, seemingly out of nowhere. That player was Codecademy. Most entrepreneurs (especially the ones in this book) understand the challenges of convincing early users to use the product, but founders Ryan Bubinski and Zach Sims blew past all of them when they launched in 2011; Codecademy picked up hundreds of thousands of users in its first forty-eight hours.

Today, the site offers interactive lessons in programming languages and frameworks, including JavaScript, Python, and Ruby. It's interesting to note the shared goal between Codecademy and General Assembly: both set out to fix the skills gap between what students were being taught in college and what industry jobs asked of them. Having competition is generally a good thing, as it validates that solving this particular problem has value.

Many founders are overly concerned with competition because they fail to realize that one company "killing" the other is far from the most probable outcome. In reality, it's much more likely that both companies will be fairly successful, or that other external forces will kill both of them. And indeed, despite the similar goal, the two companies have taken very different approaches, both of which may be viable. Codecademy is entirely digital, embodying the notion of scalability more readily than General Assembly, which plans and opens campuses one at a time.

GUO: How did Codecademy get started?

BUBINSKI: Codecademy was the product of a partnership in college between my cofounder, Zach, and me. We were a year apart at Columbia, but during the three years that we overlapped, the two of us worked on a variety of projects together.

During my senior year, some friends and I started a group on campus called the Application Development Initiative, which was similar to PennApps and other college programming groups at the time. Zach helped us work out the financing for our first hackathon in January of 2011. Two weeks later, Zach and I decided to start a company and figure out just what that would entail. We applied to Y Combinator, flew out to California, got in, and over the course of that summer worked on four or five different projects.

We spent the last three weeks of YC building the core prototype, which became the precursor to the product that exists today. Over the past three years, we've significantly grown both the product and company behind that original demo.

GUO: What were some of the other ideas that you tried?

BUBINSKI: Zach and I are intently focused on closing the skills gap in the global workforce. We both exited college smack in the middle of the aftermath of the subprime mortgage crisis.

All around us we saw this imbalance between unfilled jobs and growing unemployment numbers. It was a bit surreal—our friends who happened to major in computer science were receiving these amazing six-digit offers straight out of college while other classmates were really struggling to find opportunities postgraduation. We kept seeing firsthand just how wide this skills gap is in STEM and computer science.

If you're not embarrassed of your first product, you've waited too long to launch.

When we first applied to YC, we were building a tool to help companies conduct programming interviews, and we wanted to use that information to later build a larger data set of people with technical skills. We wanted to create a resource for companies to hire from anywhere, not just the top ten engineering schools.

We hit a wall with that approach when we realized the programmers we were after had little interest in proving their skills. This put us back at square one. In between this first iteration and Codecademy, we worked on a couple misguided projects. One was particularly horrendous. We never actually launched it, but basically we tried to build a website creator for small businesses. We got a handful of companies to commit; we built their websites, but we never had the traction nor the passion for the challenge. After four weeks, Zach and I looked at each other and said, "This really isn't for us." We decided to go back to the original challenge of helping to close the skills gap.

With the benefit of a fresh perspective, we decided to pivot from a mentality of measuring everyone's technical skill sets to thinking about how to grow everyone's technical skill sets. We realized we could actually train an entirely new labor force; we just had to do it in a way that was accessible, i.e., people could both afford and attend the offering. That granted us a very different approach than our original attempt.

GUO: What did the Codecademy launch look like?

BUBINSKI: We were very fortunate. Unlike most startups, we didn't have the typical struggle through the initial publicity bump and resulting Trough of Sorrow. Pressed for time with the Demo Day deadline approaching, we fired off a "Show HN" post, which quickly became one of the highest-ranking posts at that time. We were showing off a very early prototype of the product, but it was clear we were onto something. In general, if you're not embarrassed of your first product, you've waited too long to launch.

We put it all out there to see how people would react to a product that offered "the easiest way to learn to code for free," and the initial response was incredible. I don't remember all the specifics—it was a long time ago—but we had on the order of hundreds of thousands of users hitting the product over a period of forty-eight hours. We had to worry about scale from the very beginning. That moment was a fantastic validation of all of our effort to take a different approach to solving a universal problem.

GUO: How did you approach user growth after the launch?

BUBINSKI: After the launch, our challenge was to both discover and create the product and then the business to back up our initial success.

The most important thing we did was to get in direct contact with our customers. It's trite but true—we built the right product by actually talking and listening to our customers. It's really easy to lose sight of that. In the very beginning, every member of the team pitched in to provide support.

Even though we were offering a free service, we replied to every request by hand. We wanted to hear from as many users as possible at first. How were people reacting to this product? What did they care about? What did they want to see? How were their needs being met and, more importantly, how were their needs not being met? We wanted to learn as much as possible so we could prioritize what to build next. Listening to your customers, and prioritizing properly, is incredibly important when you're really small and you don't have a well-established model for your business. Because roadmapping is really, really hard for a new business model—a "zero-to-one" model, in the words of Peter Thiel.

As a bit of a disclaimer, I do think that the idea of doing things that don't scale is valid, but I think you either end up automating those actions or you hire people to take them over; they're rarely temporary responsibilities. A lot of those responsibilities will likely never go away; you just change your relationship to them as a founder. I don't know if it gets talked about much in this way, but I actually see unscalable things as more of a commentary on the founders' relationship to the less glamorous activities of running a business as opposed to the activities themselves.

Our content creation process has always been a mix of community volunteers, independent authors, and internal content creation. And there's a continual challenge to offer the highest-quality content offerings that we can. So it's not a tactic that "never really scales"—we just try to get better and better at solving it.

GUO: In the process of getting better at solving these problems, are there any that you've automated away?

BUBINSKI: Absolutely, I think every technology company has that trajectory of evolution. As we've created more content, we've built tools to help create the content and improve its quality.

When we first started, Zach made the first course in Codecademy while I was building out the core product. I was testing his content; he was testing my code. And that was an incredibly effective partnership, but it was an extremely manual process.

> *We put it all out there to see how people would react to a product that offered "the easiest way to learn to code for free," and the initial response was incredible. . . . We had on the order of hundreds of thousands of users hitting the product over a period of forty-eight hours.*

He would edit the content directly in a Word doc, but if you're familiar with the product, you know it's not just a text file or a video, it's an actual interactive lesson. So it's incredibly important to understand not just your teaching language, but also what experience you want to create. And the only way to get a sense of that experience is to actually put it in the product.

We went from working with Word docs to building a simple way to format lessons, which was just parsing a simple YAML file and putting that into the database. Eventually, Zach started editing files in the database directly, which is a very scary and very unscalable way of managing a site's content. But this was before we launched, and when you only have three weeks to build something, you do what you got to do.

After we launched, we upped our requirements for stability, uptime, and doing things "the right way." Of course now we no longer edit content directly in the database. We do a lot of drafting and storyboarding. Certain parts of the process still happen in a Word doc, but that's just for outlining the content. We've invested in building our increasingly better tools for that type of content production.

The most important thing we did was to get in direct contact with our customers. It's trite but true—we built the right product by actually talking and listening to our customers.

GUO: What are your thoughts on scalability moving forward?

BUBINSKI: We've done a lot of experimentation, but by definition we've always tried to scope projects as an MVP. Our initial primary goal is to answer questions about the market as opposed to building out functionality.

For any experiment you want to run, any effort to validate or invalidate an aspect of the market, you're going to do things that don't scale. You're going to cut corners. You're going to put out a simple email as opposed to a beautiful, localized email that's readable in all formats. You're going to offer a product that maybe doesn't even exist yet. You're going to provide services by hand that you would never be able to do at scale. But that's not only

---

For any experiment you want to run, any effort to validate or invalidate an aspect of the market, you're going to do things that don't scale.

---

okay, it's ideal, because what you learn from those efforts will provide answers to critical questions that will be foundational to your business.

CHAPTER 13: 99DRESSES

Nikki Durkin, Founder & CEO

9dresses has a few unique qualities among the companies in this book. For starters, it was founded overseas. Nikki Durkin started the company in 2010 after finishing high school in Sydney, Australia. Originally, the site was a marketplace for users to trade clothes and other fashion items with other users.

The company is also unique within this book because it failed (or rather, unique *for now*; the vast majority of tech startups fail, and it's very likely that other companies in this book will also die). Durkin shut down the company in 2014 after failing to replicate the company's Australian success in the United States. The press often glorifies hardship when it ultimately leads to success, but very few founders share their stories when they end in failure.

There are likely many reasons why 99dresses wasn't successful, but it's important to consider the idea of timing: 99dresses came to market at the start of the sharing economy, only a few years after Airbnb, at the same time as RelayRides (car sharing), and before companies like FlightCar (airport car sharing). It's possible that the market was not favorable enough at the time. Today, there are several similar companies in this space, including Le Tote and Rentez-Vous, and we will see if their approaches ultimately win out.

GUO: How did 99dresses get started?

DURKIN: Well, it originally started with a business that I created when I was fifteen. I would design T-shirts and have them drop-shipped from China. I sold them through eBay, and I ended up selling hundreds of shirts a month. I was making a lot of money for a schoolgirl. I didn't have any expenses; I could just go and buy clothes, so that's what I did. It was a hobby. I had just amassed all of these clothes and realized that I needed an efficient system for dealing with all of them.

I was very lucky to be a young female in tech, because I got a ton of press. I got a shitload of press without engaging any PR people.

When I was eighteen, literally the day I finished high school, I started working on this idea. This was back when you could do this on Facebook, but I created a Facebook event and said, "Hey, I'm Nikki, and I have all these clothes, but nothing to wear. Here's my idea on how to fix it," and I explained how the website worked.

Then I said, "If you think you would use something like this, could you click 'attending'? If you're interested, send it out to your friends." I sent it out to two hundred girlfriends, and within a few weeks, there were probably about forty thousand women in this event. I had thousands of fans of this nonexistent product, and from there, I collaborated with the community to figure out "What are you going to call it?" and "How is the virtual currency going to work?" and things like that. We originally launched in Australia, and it took off with no marketing spend. I was very lucky to be a young female in tech, because I got a ton of press. I got a shitload of press without engaging any PR people.

Getting to America was much more difficult, however. When we launched it in America, we relaunched over there. This was in 2013. We had a community that was really tight-knit, so we would do things like take our best members, put them in a Facebook group, collaborate with them, and just form strong personal connections with them. It was how we built up a really loyal community.

When we first started, we'd obviously list our own clothes, but we'd also go to Nordstrom and spend $10,000 at a time on tons of clothes. We'd list them, and then anything that we didn't give away or trade we'd return within the thirty-day return policy. We did stuff like that, which worked really well.

GUO: Where did your first few hundred users come from? Did they all come out of the Facebook group?

DURKIN: The Facebook group was before I had a product, and that was a very active group. People were like, "When's it coming out?" I kept them engaged by doing stuff like, "Let's do a poll on what we're going to call the virtual currency." That's how the name "buttons" came up—one of the girls in the group suggested it. We ended up building the ability to upload pictures of dresses. It started out in Australia; it was just dresses. All you could do was sign up for the website and upload dresses. You couldn't actually trade anything, because there was no point being able to trade things if no one was going to upload, because we had this massive chicken-and-egg problem.

We got some of them into a mailing list, and then when we were ready we would send out these invites. All you could do was sign up and upload dresses. We said, "When we get a thousand dresses on there, we'll open up the site for trading, and the people who sent the initial dresses will get free virtual currency to kick-start the trading." We did that; I think it took four weeks or six weeks to get the thousand dresses. Looking back, I'm surprised people did that at all, because it's really high risk. You don't know what you are trading with; you're just uploading stuff. They took the time to do that, and it wasn't an easy thing like an app back then; it was a website.

We'd also go to Nordstrom and spend $10,000 at a time on tons of clothes. We'd list them, and then anything that we didn't give away or trade we'd return within the thirty-day return policy.

They uploaded items, and when we got a thousand dresses, it opened up the trading side of things. Immediately, people had virtual currency, and they started trading. Within our first few months, we had done five thousand trades or something, with a pretty small, tight-knit community that got addicted.

GUO: Tell me more about spending $10,000 at a time at Nordstrom.

DURKIN: That was crazy, actually. It was really fun. This was when we launched our app in the US; we would go to Nordstrom Rack. They have a thirty-day return policy, and we would just go and shop and spend thousands of dollars on clothes—hundreds of items.

Then we'd photograph them, put them on a website, and it worked pretty well because it set an example. It set the example of at least decent-quality items and the expectation that you could get good-quality items and therefore *list* good-quality items.

It was just a way of seeding the site. The good thing about that is, most of it didn't end up getting traded. We'd just return it and go get new stuff. We only had to do a few cycles of that; we phased it out pretty quickly. Logistically, all of that was pretty brutal. And we didn't need to do it after four or six weeks.

It looks like we ran out of money, but that's just a symptom of the problem. It was a great product, but it was really not a good business because of the unit economics of it.

GUO: Was there anything that appeared automated to users but was done manually on your end?

DURKIN: When we launched in the US, we spent a while building out an entire system to give the appearance that we already had an active community on our app when we launched. We knew if you start a network-effect business, and you don't have what appears to be a community, it's really hard to get started. So we developed a system: we'd create all these fake personas, all these fake profiles, and they'd comment on things. We'd do that all manually—log in to the accounts and do this and that. It would automatically like posts, and you could trade things, and all these transactions had to be automated.

It would be such a logistical nightmare to do it manually, and do it well, and so we actually invested time making that software and then phasing it out as fast as we could. But it worked really, really well. It looked like we had a really active community, when in reality it was us behind the scenes. But we built tech to manage all of that in an efficient way, because if we would do that manually, it just wouldn't work. It was too much. But our users still don't really know that.

We only needed it for a few weeks, and honestly, I don't see the problem with it. I know it's kind of a gray area, but a lot of growth hacking is in a gray area, and as long as no one is being hurt by a strategy, I think it's worth a try. Without it, you can go along for ages spending all this money trying to market a product, when the only reason people aren't engaging in the product is because they think no one else is. If you're a new marketplace and you don't have that community, getting more people in the door is somewhat irrelevant. With these marketplace businesses, you really need to go off with a bang to get some kind of traction, which can build on itself. If you start off with nothing, it's really difficult to get it to take off.

GUO: How was the experience of transplanting an Australian company to the United States?

DURKIN: Very difficult. The problem is, when you're in your home country, you have friends and networks. You know the culture and all of that. Especially starting off as a marketplace, you need that. Normally, your friends will help you out; personally I got all of my friends involved. But when I went to America, I didn't know any girls, so it was really hard to do that. You don't really know the culture. Our problem was that we pushed out exactly what worked in Australia, and what worked in Australia absolutely did not work in the US.

We ended up having to pretty much scrap that product, rebuild everything, and focus on mobile. Change the way the trading system worked to make it fit in with the American market. Most people look at Australia and America and think, "Oh, it's not that different," but culturally, just in terms of competition, things were much more fierce in America. This psychology of online shopping is also quite different, so we had to really cater to that.

I had this belief that it would be fun and easy, and it was fun and easy. . . . But I started believing it was really hard, and I had to work really hard, and I killed myself working on the startup and made things really, really difficult.

GUO: Knowing what you know now, could you adapt the company if you did it again?

DURKIN: Not with 99dresses. That was the reason we failed. It looks like we ran out of money, but that's just a symptom of the problem. It was a great product, but it was really not a good business because of the unit economics of it.

We were solving a big problem in a way that was great for the environment, and great for our loyal community, but it's hard to make money from a peer-to-peer marketplace for one-off, low-value items. What we were doing, girls loved it, but you're making a couple of bucks on a secondhand fashion item. The unit economics of making it scale out is just not that compelling compared to other things you could be doing. It was hard to see that when you've got so much riding on it, and are so passionate about it, but that was what I saw.

GUO: What's something that you've learned from the successes and failures of your business?

DURKIN: In general, things worked so much better when I stopped trying so hard. I could get so stressed out about coming up with the right strategy, doing this and doing that, but things just worked for me in really lucky sets of coincidences when I wasn't trying so hard.

I had this belief that it would be fun and easy, and it *was* fun and easy. Everything just lined up in the beginning. I had this Facebook group, and some of the coincidences that happened allowed me to grow that, and launch it, and attract all these people. But I started believing it was really hard, and I had to work really hard, and I killed myself working on the startup and made things really, really difficult.

CHAPTER 14: WATSI

Grace Garey, Cofounder & Head of Marketing

Watsi is a nonprofit crowdfunding site that lets anyone directly fund low-cost, high-impact medical care for people in need. It stands out as the only nonprofit in this book, and it was the first nonprofit accepted into Y Combinator. Watsi was founded by Grace Garey, Chase Adam, and Jesse Cooke in 2012, and like Tilt and Teespring, applied crowdfunding technology to a new vertical—medical care, in this instance.

Despite its nonprofit status, the company faces many of the same challenges as other startups. Like ZeroCater, Teespring, FlightCar, and DoorDash, Watsi was held together for a long time with spreadsheets, emails, and duct tape; the founders created automated processes only as their existing ones became too difficult to support. In fact, they likely did this more often than those other companies, as Watsi has had only one developer on staff for the majority of its existence.

GUO: Tell me about how you met your cofounders and how you first got started with Watsi.

GAREY: So my cofounder Chase used to be in the Peace Corps, and while he was volunteering in Costa Rica, a woman boarded a bus he was on, trying to pay for her son's health care by asking passengers for donations. When he came back from the Peace Corps, he had the idea of a Kiva for health care, and he started working on Watsi on the side. Jesse, our first developer, volunteered to work on it with him, and for the first year and a half of the organization, we were all volunteering on top of our day jobs.

Before we had our website, no one could really donate. That whole first year was spent thinking and planning, with Jesse slowly building the website. We did a tiny project a few months before the launch, where we accepted three initial patients from our partner in Nepal and had our friends and family donate to make sure everything worked.

When we launched, nothing really happened. Our parents donated, but not much else. So we decided to post a link on Hacker News saying, "We just built a site that saves lives," and the amount of traffic that it drove crashed the site.

Eventually, when we launched, nothing really happened. Our parents donated, but not much else. So we decided to post a link on Hacker News saying, "We just built a site that saves lives," and the amount of traffic that it drove crashed the site. Once we got it back up, we managed to fund the health care for every patient that we had posted.

But the process of handling all of those was pretty ridiculous. I was writing patient profiles from the bathroom of my day job on my phone and forwarding them to Steve so he could forward them to Stephanie, who would hard code them into the site, because we didn't have a CRM.

GUO: Where did your first dozen patients come from?

GAREY: Our first health care partners came from friends and connections that we had. Chase and I had both lived and worked in various countries before, and we went through and scanned our entire friends list, emails, LinkedIn, for any connections to any of the world's best hospitals or health organizations. We reached out to them, and we ended up bringing three initial hospitals on board: one in Ethiopia, one in Guatemala, and one in Nepal. Which is how we got our first patient profile. And our network of medical providers grew in a similar way; it was almost all through recommendations from those partners.

GUO: How have you managed growth since then?

GAREY: I think in the near future, we will scale out the patient side somewhat. One thing was that we were dealing with a high volume of patients early on, but there were only three of us working on Watsi full time. Our patient volume was doubling or tripling every week, but I was still writing every single patient profile by hand, and every single update was being copied and pasted from an email that the medical partner sent.

There was no online form or anything for a medical partner to submit a patient to Watsi. They would send a Word document with an attached photo to my Gmail account. And I would open up the Word document and the privacy waiver, and I'd download it, upload it, copy it, and write a version of the patient profile that would go up on our website. We would do the same thing for our patient updates so we could tell donors when the patient was actually receiving heath care. But as our volume grew, our process did not get any better, so we were adding more hours to the day.

At one point we asked a mentor for advice, because we didn't know how to prioritize things; we didn't know what to focus on, what to do first, how to finish all of those things. And he told us,

---

I was writing patient profiles from the bathroom of my day job on my phone and forwarding them to Steve so he could forward them to Stephanie, who would hard code them into the site, because we didn't have a CRM.

"Just work harder." So we were working twenty-hour days, there was so much manual labor to be done.

Another thing was until recently we manually published all of our financials, all of our operations information, in a Google spreadsheet. We called it our "transparency document." Now it's almost entirely automated, but for the first year and a half of Watsi, we filled in twenty rows of information for every patient that we had. We tracked the patient's age, who submitted them, their treatment cost, their acceptance date, and tons of other numbers. We also had to duplicate this work for our medical partners so they could each have a list of only their patients, with information on which ones were outstanding or had pending updates.

And all of that was completely manually entered into this spreadsheet, and it's something that Watsi donors and people really love. They love that we say we're transparent and we actually are; you can see screenshots of some transfers from our bank account to our medical partners. But upholding that value is something that is really important to us, and taking the time to keep up with that and maintain that spreadsheet was a way for us to put our money where our mouths were.

GUO: Walk me through the patient onboard process.

GAREY: A patient will walk into the hospital and be diagnosed with something really serious, and they don't have enough money to pay for it. So the doctors, the hospital will identify them as a potentially good candidate for Watsi. They explain Watsi to the patient and ask if they want to interview, and if the patient agrees, a doctor records the interview on a physical sheet of paper. We have a set of questions that we ask for critical information about the patient and information about their life outside of their medical condition.

Then they either scan the paper or type it into a Word document, and along with a photo of the patient they upload the patient's information. In the early days they would email that information to me, and I would get that email and I would open it up, and make sure it looked good, and that the medical condition and everything met our high-level criteria, and I would send an email back saying, "Yes, this patient has been approved, and we will put them on Watsi until they are fully funded."

Then I would take all of the content from the Word document and information about the patient and format it into a story, a profile for the patient, to go on the site. I'd download their photo and crop it according to our site requirements, and they would be put into our admin back end, ready to be posted to the website.

The one tool that we've been using since the early days that we still use today is Trello. We use it to track more contextual information on a patient. Every single patient has a card on Trello; it's where we go to comment and make notes. If we get a call or email from a doctor about a patient's care being delayed, or if we are saving certain patients for a specific fundraiser and we don't want them to be published on the website, all of the patient updates are tracked in Trello.

GUO: How have some of those manual processes changed?

GAREY: One of the biggest differences is that we are no longer receiving new patient profiles via email. There is an online form now that partners have access to, and they can fill out and submit a patient to Watsi with the click of a button. The patients show up in our back end, and also they show up on Trello so that we can approve them on our end.

A lot of the content is still very manual; it's just a larger team of people now. So while I physically wrote the first thousand patient profiles on Watsi, we now have a team of about twenty writing volunteers to help us do all of that. But we're still in a place where to format the image for the website, volunteers are still downloading the original image from the medical partner and opening up Photoshop or something to do it themselves, and so we just hired an engineer about two weeks ago whose first project is working on putting an image cropper in our back end, so you can crop the image right there. So there are some improvements, definitely.

GUO: As a nonprofit, how do you approach finding volunteers?

GAREY: We get a lot of people that want to reach out to us and want to learn how they can get involved. That's a good place for us to throw out what our needs are and find out if they're interested in volunteering. We get an assortment of recent grads, people that work in a medical field, people that have after-hours times or weekends that have a little bit more flexibility. Generally we deal with people who write for a living, and since most of it is medical content curation, we have copywriters and junior copywriters that write as volunteers.

We get people who have established careers or are looking for something more engaging to do, or people who love Watsi's mission, or recent grads or students who are looking for a resume builder. As our hiring program has gotten up and running, a lot of volunteers refer their friends, which is wonderful, so we actually have a waiting list now of volunteers who want to help write Watsi patient profiles who we actually can't accommodate right now, which is a great problem to have.

Right now, we have seven full-time staff. We have three engineers, one designer, one medical operations person, me, and Chase. On top of that we have about twenty volunteers. Most of those volunteers are remote; a few of them are in our office a cou-

---

At one point we asked a mentor for advice, because we didn't know how to prioritize things; we didn't know what to focus on, what to do first, how to finish all of those things. And he told us, "Just work harder." So we were working twenty-hour days, there was so much manual labor to be done.

---

ple days a week, but most of them are just part of a remote program that we manage.

GUO: How do you go above and beyond for your users?

GAREY: So like other teams, one thing we have done is send handwritten thank-you notes—especially around Thanksgiving and during the holidays—to various donors, whether it's some of the earliest donors who joined, or people that have given a lot of money to patients, or people who have told a lot of their friends about Watsi. We try to surprise them with little handwritten notes in packages around the holidays.

With patients the typical experience for a Watsi donor is that you sign up, you donate to a patient, and then maybe a couple weeks later after they receive health care, you get an update on that patient and how they're doing, and have this established process and mark the case as closed. We don't have any obligation or anything after we've sent that final update to all of the donors, but sometimes six months later, we'll get an amazing photo from a medical partner saying, "Maria came back from the hospital; look how well she's doing! She's walking now; just thought you guys would like to see her."

When that happens, we'll go back and dig through the archives and send another email thanking a few of the donors who helped fund that patient's care. We will sort of manually send an email out, and say, "Hey, we thought you'd love to see this. Look at what you helped to make possible." And they really appreciate that Watsi sort of operates as more of a human being than a company. Just the fact that it's not exactly our obligation, not something we have to provide them, but we just think it makes sense.

The whole goal of Watsi is to connect people to each other, and so when something happens in one person's life that someone else made possible, we want to keep that connection going even if it's hard to add that to the list of things to do.

CHAPTER 15: GITHUB

Tom Preston-Werner, Cofounder

Nowadays, software developers consider GitHub an indispensable tool, one that is sometimes used as a replacement resume. But that hasn't always been the case. GitHub became a staple of programming over the last eight years, after being founded in 2008 by Tom Preston-Werner and Chris Wanstrath.

It's likely that every company in this book has used GitHub at one point or another. Why is it so popular? Because it greatly improved the way the world shares code, via online Git repository hosting. And while there are many technologies for tracking software changes and moving code across computers, GitHub made it a social experience, and the company gave away its product to open-source-software contributors.

Although it is one of the largest companies in this book, GitHub was almost entirely bootstrapped (the company raised $100 million four years after its founding). It's a company by Silicon Valley engineers for Silicon Valley engineers, but it avoided the heavily funded rocket ship route. This is an important observation, as it shows us that raising mountains of venture capital is not a one-size-fits-all model.

GUO: So how did you and Chris [Wanstrath] first meet? Where did you get the idea for GitHub?

PRESTON-WERNER: Well, we met through the Ruby users group that was here in San Francisco. We would go to conferences, and I saw him talk and we'd always talk about Git. This was back when Git was still very hard to use, but it was really bubbling in the air, around the Ruby on Rails community especially.

And we were extremely lucky to have Rails come on board, to switch over from their existing version control system when we publicly launched. . . . That alone maybe made GitHub possible at all.

People were starting to pay attention to it, but nobody really knew what to do with it because it was so hard to use. And we were experimenting with it a little bit at my job. When I first saw it, I thought, "This is obviously the future of version control."

But there was only one website where you could share repositories, and it was quite bad, so I said, "I'm a web developer. Why don't I build a website to make it easier to share, with a central repository so that people don't have to set up their own servers and create user accounts and all these kinds of things?"

At the time, Chris had also been thinking a lot about Git and how to use it, and we had already worked together on another project, a process monitor in Ruby. So we knew how bad the experience of sharing code via Git was because of that project.

I wanted to do it with Chris because I knew him through the Ruby community. So after one of the meetups—we met at a bar, as we often did—I showed Chris a project I had started working on. It was a Git wrapper in Ruby that was called Grit. I showed it to him and I kind of pitched him my idea and said, "Are you interested?" And he said, "Yeah! I'm in." So we just started hacking on it on nights and weekends.

I wanted him to do the [Ruby on] Rails stuff. I thought I could do the visual design and back end, and he could do the Rails app, and the two of us would make a really good team because of that complementary skill set.

GUO: Where did your initial users come from?

PRESTON-WERNER: It took about three months before we launched the private beta, so it wasn't a long wait. It was a very, very basic product at first, as you can imagine. It was just two people working on it nights and weekends for three months.

We started showing it to people at Ruby meetups, since they were our friends. They were the people we would hang out with. In fact, back then a lot of people from Twitter, and Engine Yard, and Powerset were there. That was the kind of crew here in San Francisco.

So we'd show it around. We were like, "Hey, we're doing this code-sharing thing, and you can have Git repositories and put them up there." We gave out invites to the people at the meetups, and we told them that they could invite other people through our private system.

So that's how we got our original users. They were just through the existing Ruby community that we knew. And that's why GitHub started with the Ruby community, because it happened to be the community we were a part of.

And we were *extremely* lucky to have Rails come on board, to switch over from their existing version control system when we publicly launched. That was in April of 2008, which was about six months after we started coding. And that was huge for us. That alone maybe made GitHub possible at all.

GUO: How did you get DHH (David Heinemeier Hansson) and the Rails team to switch?

> *I think that was the really big thing that allowed GitHub to become popular very easily. There was almost no barrier to entry to getting code on GitHub.*

PRESTON-WERNER: We emailed them and tried to explain why we thought they should switch to GitHub, probably four or five months in. And they responded and said, "No thanks!"

And then over the next month or two, or however long it was, they started seeing other people using GitHub. And actually it was Merb that was our first milestone. Merb was the first prominent Ruby project to switch over. It was Ezra [Zygmuntowicz]'s and Yehuda Katz's project, and they were two of our very first users. So Merb switched over officially to Git, and that preceded Rails by a couple of months. And I think that was the first thing that got people to raise their eyebrows and say, "Oh, interesting. An actual real project is using GitHub."

Although now probably nobody knows what Merb even is anymore, but at the time it was a lightweight alternative to Rails. Remember, we had emailed the Rails guys and they had rejected us. But I think over the next couple of months they saw more and more people using GitHub, enough projects, to where they started getting comfortable with the idea of it. They probably started playing with it. And once you start playing with Git, especially in combination with GitHub, then there's no turning back from there. It's just too good; it's too awesome. Git is just too awesome.

So Rails switched to using GitHub. That single event was really momentous in our adoption. Because what it did was, it made everyone in the Rails community almost overnight switch to using Git and GitHub as their version control.

GUO: Why was that?

PRESTON-WERNER: People are going to use whatever their favorite projects use. You need to know the version control system that your tools are using, in order to contribute. And other people use that as a signal to know what they should be using for their packages, for their plug-ins, for things that are going to be useful for frameworks.

And because the Ruby on Rails community were such early adopters—it was in their very nature of having chosen to use Ruby on Rails at the time—it made it so that they were willing to try GitHub, to make a change without worrying about it too much. So that's how we got our original set of users. It was just the Ruby community and then through Rails.

GUO: Did you try to recruit other projects to GitHub?

PRESTON-WERNER: Yeah, there was a phase where we emailed a bunch of project maintainers and pitched them and asked them if they were interested in moving their projects to GitHub, but it wasn't super successful. We tried jQuery; at one point one of us emailed John Resig about getting jQuery to switch over. And that was unsuccessful for several years!

And you know we would come in contact with him, and kind of joke with him about how he should switch over, and eventually they switched over all of the jQuery plug-ins, I think. There was something that they switched over, but they didn't switch over the jQuery core for years. Mostly because they didn't want to alienate their significant base of Subversion contributors. But eventually they relented.

Most of the project maintainers early on said, "Sorry, we can't switch because of all our Subversion contributors." And with the Ruby core itself, we talked to the core developers there about switching. When I was at conferences with any of the Ruby core people, I would always bring it up. But what we found was that it's impossible to convince project maintainers to switch. They have to convince themselves.

You have to also realize, though, that the GitHub team grew extremely slowly in the beginning. After three years, we were a team of six people.

GUO: Was Subversion the most common roadblock?

PRESTON-WERNER: Yeah, that was almost always the reason. With smaller projects, they would just switch over of their own accord, and you didn't have to convince anyone. At least in the Ruby and JavaScript communities, you knew that would just happen naturally.

But for the ones that had a real reason not to switch to Git and GitHub, it was Subversion. Or in the case of something like Linux, it was that they already had an existing process with their work flow and it would be too disruptive for them to try to change. Linux has a very heavy mailing list–based work flow. The way they accept patches is through the mailing list, and all the discussion happens there, and they have systems for dealing with that. The amount of infrastructure that they have built up is too vast to switch to another system.

And obviously the Linux kernel has always used Git since Git was created. So they are using Git, but they just couldn't use GitHub because of work flow.

GUO: How has the sign-up process for GitHub changed since then?

PRESTON-WERNER: Actually, it's primarily unchanged. Really all you need to do is create a repository on GitHub, on your account, and then push to it from the command line or from whatever tool.

At the time there was only the command-line client. There were no graphical interfaces for a long time. Now you can use any of the graphical interfaces that are available: GitHub for Mac, GitHub for Windows, Git Tower. There are a ton of them now. So those are new channels that you can use, but the way you create a repository on GitHub is essentially unchanged.

There is a difference in that now you can create a new project on GitHub that is already initialized and has a README so that you can clone it. You haven't always been able to do that. You'd have to create the repository on your local side and then push it. So that's a little bit handy, but it's really not much different.

I think that was the really big thing that allowed GitHub to become popular very easily. There was almost no barrier to entry to getting code on GitHub, whereas with other hosting services you'd have to go through an application and approval process to even get a place where you could put your code. It was a very high barrier to entry to put your code online with them.

And then places like Google Code were okay. You didn't have to get permission, but it was still a single namespace, a global namespace, and it was project based. You also had to choose an open source license, which was another barrier. Because when a lot of people put up code, they're not in the mind-set to choose licenses and things. And I don't think that you should force someone to choose a license just because they're putting some code online. I don't think that's appropriate.

So we've always taken the stance that you don't have to choose a license if you don't want to. We want to make it easy for you to do that, because we think it's best practice to choose a license so that others are clear about what that license is and how to use your code. But we never wanted to force that on people, and by reducing the amount of choice there was, we made it easier for people to do it. We tried to reduce how much they had to think about it. It was like, just push whatever code you have onto GitHub and you know you'll never lose it again. You can just share it when you want to share it.

GUO: As a pure software company, what things did you have to do manually?

PRESTON-WERNER: Well, the company was all about using technology to serve people building technology. And the people using it understood what that meant, and everyone who was using it in the early days had to be sophisticated enough to know what it was in the first place, which meant that they were probably sophisticated enough to know how to run the basic commands and to get their code up.

The things we had to do manually were in tech support, which we did as a team. We all did support. We all did support for many, many years. We hired our first full-time support person probably two years in.

You have to also realize, though, that the GitHub team grew extremely slowly in the beginning. After three years, we were a team of six people. We weren't one of those heavily funded startups that grows to one hundred people in year one. That just wasn't our path.

We were bootstrapped, and we were letting people adapt to Git at a natural pace. We couldn't really force people to use Git; it was impossible. People had to desire to learn it on their own and had to desire to use it on their own. And so we didn't do a ton of marketing. Everything we did in marketing was unscalable, as the marketing that we did do was basically going to conference talks. We did a lot of conference talks.

And that included the founders. We would spent a lot of time traveling, especially internationally. We gave talks about Git to help people learn how to use it and to talk about us as a company and what we were doing. And that was definitely unscalable from a founder perspective.

We were lucky in [the] early days of GitHub that there were no regulations that we were up against. There weren't incumbents that had to be battled in that way.

We always wanted GitHubbers to be able to travel and give conference talks. So we always had a policy that if you ever got a speaking slot at a conference, GitHub would pay for you to go there and give a talk. So we scaled out the conference talks by distributing that out to the entire company.

We also did drinkups, which were essentially meetups at bars. It came from the idea that one of our favorite parts of the Ruby meetups was the meeting with people afterwards at a bar to drink and talk about technology, and it was a place where people could just share ideas freely. During the meetup itself it was much more structured. People could get quite impatient, and it was usually one person talking to a lot of people versus everyone talking to each other.

So we always really enjoyed the part of the meetups where you'd be able to talk to everyone. And that was either afterwards at a bar or some other venue, and we'd get a couple of kegs or whatever, and we'd sit wherever the meetup was and we'd hang out. So we decided to try to replicate that experience with our own users.

That worked really well. It was awesome. We got a ton of people who would come out, and they'd have a really great time talking about technology. In the early days, they had enough in common that the conversations would always be really good. You always had in common that you were a GitHub user, which probably meant that you were using Ruby or JavaScript or another dynamic language, because in the early days there were only a small number of languages that were really prominent on GitHub.

So it was a way for us to do what I called "creating superfans," which meant going above and beyond what was expected from the company in order to surprise and delight the customers. We wanted to increase loyalty, to help them understand that we're real humans, that we care about what they care about. And we wanted them to know that they had a venue where they could interact with us and let us know how the product was working for them, and what features they wanted and what they were doing with it.

So it was an awesome channel. And I went to every drinkup that we had locally, or wherever I was where there was a drinkup. I went to almost every single one for probably three years, here in San Francisco. In the early days, when we first started them, we did them every week at first. And then we switched to every two weeks and eventually we switched to monthly. But I went to an incredible number of the drinkups to be able to meet our users.

I think that could probably count as something that didn't scale in the long run, although I managed to pull it off for quite a while.

GUO: What did the growth curve look like at the time?

PRESTON-WERNER: Growth was always pretty steady. There was never a moment in time where there was a crazy inflection point. It was just a steady long-term exponential growth curve. And I think that was because it took a lot for people to switch to using Git.

It's not a trivial thing to ask a company to switch their version control system. Most companies have a lot of infrastructure built around their deployment system and CI [continuous integration], and all of their developers are trained to use something. To ask them to switch that, and all their projects and everything, to a new version control system is very high cost. So the larger the company, the longer it takes them to do it, because of the inherent risk in changing that.

That's a change that they are willing to consider doing maybe once every decade. And so that's why I think the growth was slow and steady like that, because it was such a high-impact change to a lot of people. As new startups were created and new open source projects were started, they could just choose GitHub from the beginning. And that became more and more easy as time went on.

And then you'd have projects like CoffeeScript or Homebrew that were born on GitHub. These are things that existed in perfect symbiosis with GitHub from their very birth. And we started seeing those and that was pretty amazing. Homebrew manages all of their recipes through GitHub. Everything they do is on

GitHub and handled through GitHub. And that's built into the core mechanisms of their software, which was very cool to see.

GUO: What scaling challenges did you have on the technical side?

PRESTON-WERNER: We were hosted on Engine Yard originally, for many years. And they were amazing; they really helped us succeed, and we had a partnership with them. We put their logo in our site footer and they gave us unlimited hosting, and that allowed us to work really well in a bootstrap fashion because we were not paying as much for hosting.

So we used them for a long time, but their global file system was Red Hat GFS [Global File System], so all the Rails servers would basically mount GFS as a drive and all of the Git repositories would be accessible through that one drive. So every front-end server didn't have to care that the storage was not local. It would just make believe that it was local.

The problem, though, was once we got enough front ends, there started to be a lot of contention for those files, and the lock contention started to cause performance problems.

Somewhere between the second and third year, we started bottlenecking a lot because of that architecture. I spent a lot of time, probably around six months, re-architecting the entire site to be able to run on a distributed system where the storage was no longer local and was accessed through an RPC [remote procedure call] mechanism.

There's a blog post I wrote called "How We Made GitHub Fast," which details how I went about doing that. I completely re-architected how the back end works to allow us to use commodity Linux servers as the storage nodes along with separate servers to act as front ends. That allowed any front end to contact any back end and be able to find where the repositories were stored.

We deployed that on Rackspace, and we also had a partnership with them to get discounted storage for putting their logo in our footer. We did those partnerships early on because it was a win-win. These companies got advertising and we got cheaper hosting. We did that for many years, but eventually we stopped.

But yes, there was a massive re-architect that had to happen for this site to continue, or it would've gone out of business. Reliability started to suffer; I mean anyone who was around at the time would remember that phase. It was not awesome. But we were working our asses off in order to get the new architecture in place, which was a significant amount of work. And I wrote probably a half dozen open-source projects to get it done.

GUO: What other serious hurdles did the company face early on?

PRESTON-WERNER: Performance was the primary one. There was also trust. If we were to have a serious security breach, that could be an existential crisis for the company. Those were big ones for us.

We were lucky in [the] early days of GitHub that there were no regulations that we were up against. There weren't incumbents that had to be battled in that way.

ACKNOWLEDGMENTS

First and foremost, thanks to all of the founders who took the time to do these interviews. There literally would be no book without them.

A huge, heartfelt thank-you to Alexey, Casey, Eva, Erin, Molly, Rob, Runi, Ruth, and the rest of the Hacker Paradise crew. This entire project started off as a half-baked blog post, and they helped incubate, build, and refine the idea along the way.

Lastly, thanks to the Inkshares team for turning bits into atoms and making this book a real-world reality.

ABOUT THE AUTHOR

Photo © 2015 Juan Carlos Foust

Charlie Guo lives in the San Francisco Bay Area, in the heart of the world he portrays. A software engineer by trade, he has also founded two companies. While getting his undergrad at Stanford, he started the education tech company ClassOwl. ClassOwl partners with Stanford and other schools to improve student-teacher communication and productivity, and in startup-storybook fashion it was sold by Guo's cofounders in 2015 to Branch Metrics. After graduation, he started a second company, FanHero, which was accepted into Y Combinator, a prestigious startup accelerator program based in Silicon Valley. His own experiences working to make his ideas fly exposed him to the inner workings of the startup culture and inspired him to reach out to a fascinating mix of tech founders to share their experiences.

GLOSSARY

API: Application programming interface. The interface that allows third-party software developers to build on top of an existing product or service. Many technology companies have APIs, which allow new applications to be built with their data.

BASES: Business Association of Stanford Entrepreneurial Students

chicken-and-egg problem: Most marketplaces have what is known as a "chicken-and-egg" problem. Traditionally, there are two sides of a marketplace, buyers and sellers, and you need both to get the marketplace to work. However, when you're first starting your business, you have to figure out how to get both sides (or, more likely, how to get one side and convince it to stick around long enough for the other side to show up) and which one is going to come first. Hence, chicken and egg.

CRM: Customer relationship management. Generally speaking, a product used to manage customer contacts.

David Heinemeier Hansson: A Danish programmer and creator of the Ruby on Rails web framework. He is also a partner at Basecamp (formerly 37signals) and known to the Ruby community as "DHH."

Demo Day: An invite-only event for active investors to view presentations from the latest batch of companies to come out of an accelerator. In the case of YC (*see* Y Combinator), Demo Day occurs at the end of the twelve-week program.

Engine Yard: A cloud-hosting company that is still active.

Git: If you're not familiar with Git, here's a horrendous oversimplification: Git is a technology that lets you keep track of changes to your files (*see* version control), revert to older files as necessary, and share your changes with other users. Each group of tracked files is known as a "repository."

hackathon: An event, typically lasting several days, in which a large number of people collaborate on various software or hardware projects. It's often set up as a high-intensity environment with judges and prizes.

Hacker News (HN): An Internet forum affiliated with YC (*see* Y Combinator). Users can submit links to websites or articles and have discussions.

Homebrew: A command-line package installer for OS X.

jQuery: An incredibly popular JavaScript library written by John Resig. It is currently used by over 60 percent of the world's top one hundred thousand websites.

MailChimp: A product for creating and managing email newsletters.

meatspace: The physical world, as opposed to cyberspace or a virtual environment.

MVP: Minimum viable product. Popularized by the lean startup movement, an MVP is the product with the fewest features that can collect feedback from users.

Paul Graham (PG): The founder of Y Combinator. Previously sold Internet startup Viaweb to Yahoo.

PennApps: A semiannual hackathon held at the University of Pennsylvania, which helped set off a boom of college hackathons across the country. As of 2015, over 1,500 students have come together to hack for more than $46,000 in prizes.

pivot: The act of changing a company's direction in search of traction or validation. While pivoting was originally intended to reflect small changes within a product category (such as Teleborder pivoting from a generalized legal marketplace to a focus on immigration law), in recent years it has been used to label much larger changes, even those that throw out an old business entirely and start over with a wholly new product.

Powerset: A natural language search engine for the Internet; it was acquired by Microsoft in 2008 for an estimated $100 million.

README: A README (or readme) is a file that contains information about other files in a directory or archive. Generally included as part of software documentation.

SEO: Search engine optimization. The process of improving the visibility of a website in a search engine's results.

Series A: A Series A round is the name usually given to a company's first significant round of venture capital funding. Additional rounds after the Series A are typically labeled as "Series B," "Series C," etc.

Skillshare: An online learning community to master real-world skills from project-based classes.

Subversion: An alternative version-control system to Git.

Trello: An online productivity and project-management tool based around the Japanese *kanban* system; cards are used to track the progress of different tasks through a multistep process.

Trough of Sorrow: As defined by Paul Graham (*see above*), this is the time period after the novelty of working on a startup has worn off, but before meaningful growth or success.

version control: A system that records changes to a file or set of files over time, allowing different versions to be recalled later.

vertical: In this context, *verticals* refer to different industries or areas of specialization. For example, this book contains crowdfunding companies across three different verticals: T-shirts, health care, and general money-pooling.

YAML: A data serialization format that was designed for human readability. Originally an acronym for "Yet Another Markup Language," which was later changed to "YAML Ain't Markup Language."

Y Combinator (YC): A seed fund and startup accelerator, founded in 2005. It provides seed money, advice, and connections to startups in exchange for 7 percent equity.

Yehuda Katz: Previously a core contributor to the Ruby on Rails framework, currently a cocreator of Ember.js as well as a core contributor to the Rust language.

zero-to-one model: Peter Thiel, notable entrepreneur and venture capitalist, has put forward the idea of two types of company models: a zero-to-one model (where the company creates truly innovative technologies and markets) and a one-to-n model (where the company is scaling an existing technology or cornering an existing market).

LIST OF PATRONS

This book was made possible in part by the following grand patrons who preordered the book on Inkshares.com. Thank you.

Bharath D. Sreenath
Christiana Hay
Geoffrey Bernstein
James J. Beshara
Jesse Clayburgh
Jimmy "Swift" Chen
Jose M. Rodriguez
Josh Taylor
Justin R. Kelly
Laura De La Paz
Liang Guo
Men Cheol Jeong
Panayiotis Kalaritis
Patrick Labbett
Prabhakar Gopalan
Qi Su
Raju Penmasta
Ross Sylvester
Sharon Li
Viola Li
Zach Kagin

INKSHARES

Inkshares is a crowdfunded book publisher. We democratize publishing by having readers select the books we publish—we edit, design, print, distribute, and market any book that meets a preorder threshold.

Interested in making a book idea come to life? Visit inkshares.com to find new book projects or to start your own.